CHOOSING STATE SUPREME COURT JUSTICES

CHOOSING STATE SUPREME COURT JUSTICES

Merit Selection and the Consequences of Institutional Reform

GREG GOELZHAUSER

TEMPLE UNIVERSITY PRESS
Philadelphia • *Rome* • *Tokyo*

TEMPLE UNIVERSITY PRESS
Philadelphia, Pennsylvania 19122
www.temple.edu/tempress

Library of Congress Cataloging-in-Publication Data

Names: Goelzhauser, Greg, author.
Title: Choosing state supreme court justices : merit selection and the
consequences of institutional reform / Greg Goelzhauser.
Description: Philadelphia : Temple University Press, 2016. | Includes
bibliographical references and index.
Identifiers: LCCN 2015039137| ISBN 9781439913390 (hardback (alk.
paper)) | ISBN 9781439913406 (paper (alk. paper)) |
ISBN 9781439913413 (e-book)
Subjects: LCSH: Judges—Selection and appointment—United States—
States. | Judges—United States—States—Election. | Courts of last
resort—United States—States. | Judicial process—United States—
States. | Political questions and judicial power—United States—States.
| BISAC: POLITICAL SCIENCE / Government / Judicial Branch. |
LAW / Judicial Power.
Classification: LCC KF8776 .G64 2016 | DDC 347.73/13—dc23 LC
record available at http://lccn.loc.gov/2015039137

♾ The paper used in this publication meets the requirements of the
American National Standard for Information Sciences—Permanence of
Paper for Printed Library Materials, ANSI Z39.48-1992

Printed in the United States of America

9 8 7 6 5 4 3 2 1

To Nicole, my favorite

Contents

Tables and Figures

TABLES

FIGURES

Acknowledgments

Thanks go to Madelyn Fife, Kaylee Johnson, Kyle Wallace, and Sarah Williams for excellent research assistance. Madelyn in particular waded deep into the morass of researching state supreme court justices, and the project benefited considerably as a result. Numerous people graciously responded to inquiries about biographical details regarding particular state supreme court justices, including Daniel Cordova, Scott Deleve, Gene Kelley, Claire Marumoto, Dennis Ogawa, and Phala Riffel. For making their lists of state supreme court justices publicly available through various databases, I thank Adam Bonica, Paul Brace, Kathleen Bratton, Matthew Hall, Melinda Gann Hall, Rorie Spill Solberg, Jason Windett, and Michael Woodruff. Several entities at Utah State University provided financial support, including the Department of Political Science, the College of Humanities and Social Sciences, and the Center for Women and Gender.

A previous version of Chapter 3 was presented at the 2014 annual meeting of the American Political Science Association and the associated Pre-conference on State Politics, Political Institutions, and the Executive—both in Washington, D.C.; a previous version of Chapter 4 was presented at the 2015 annual meeting of the Southern

Political Science Association in New Orleans, Louisiana; and a previous version of Chapter 5 was presented at the 2015 annual meeting of the Western Political Science Association in Las Vegas, Nevada. Thanks go to participants at those conferences for helpful feedback. I am particularly indebted to Brent Boyea and Rebecca Gill for providing extensive comments and suggestions that significantly improved the manuscript. I also thank the anonymous reviewers for their encouragement and helpful feedback.

I benefited from conversations about this project with Charles Barrilleaux, Colin Flint, Bob Howard, Peter McNamara, and Tony Peacock. Two people deserve special thanks. Chris Bonneau generously provided feedback, encouragement, and advice at various points during the project's development. And Damon Cann did the same. I am particularly grateful to Damon for paying the additional cost imparted by being just across the hallway when questions or thoughts about this project arose. His friendship resulted in a better book and simplified the process considerably.

The Temple University Press team has been a pleasure to work with. Thanks go to the staff for making this a smooth and enjoyable experience. My editor, Aaron Javsicas, has been truly exceptional. I am much obliged to Aaron for his regular encouragement, helpful feedback, and prompt responses to even the most mundane questions.

And then there's Nicole Vouvalis. Nicole offered helpful feedback on the entire manuscript, readily engaged my musings about judicial selection institutions during its development, and helped wade through law reviews looking for mastheads during multiple Las Vegas excursions. I might have written a similar book without her, but I'm glad I didn't have to.

CHOOSING STATE SUPREME COURT JUSTICES

1 | INTRODUCTION

Merit selection for state supreme court justices is one of the most important institutional innovations of the last century. Under merit selection, a commission—often comprising some combination of judges, attorneys, and the general public—is tasked with considering applications from candidates vying to fill a judicial vacancy. After reviewing applications, the commission's ostensible goal is to forward the best-available candidates to the governor, who then decides whom to appoint to the bench.[1] Amid America's long history of selecting judges by elite appointment or popular elections, merit selection for state supreme court justices made its institutional debut in 1940. Since 1940, more than half of all states have adopted merit selection to choose at least some of their state supreme court justices. Moreover, this institutional reform remains at the forefront of the public policy debate over judicial selection, with numerous states currently debating whether to adopt or abolish merit selection. After using merit selection to select supreme court justices for more than half a century, for example, serious efforts are under way in Kansas to switch to unilateral gubernatorial appointment.[2] And after using partisan elections to select supreme court justices for nearly a century, various stakeholders are debating whether to adopt merit selection in Pennsylvania.[3]

As policy makers and other stakeholders continue debating merit selection's efficacy, it is important to understand how this selection mechanism works in relation to alternative institutional arrangements for choosing judges. The overarching argument for merit selection is that it insulates judicial selection decisions from political pressure. As a result of this insulation, proponents contend, merit selection yields better-qualified judges than other selection systems. Indeed, the implication that merit selection yields better-qualified judges is built into the name such that the proposition seems true by definition. As the longtime merit selection advocacy group American Judicature Society put it, "It is called 'merit selection' because the judicial nomination commission chooses applicants on the basis of their qualifications, not on the basis of political or social connections" (American Judicature Society, n.d.).[4] Critics, however, claim that merit selection is at best a "propagandistic misnomer" (Dimino 2004, 803) and a "sound bite that . . . bears no relation to reality" (Phenicie 2012). For every claim that "merit selection produces judges who are, on the whole, better qualified and less political" (Salomon and Rubens 1992, 21), another finds "no evidence that merit selection produces higher quality judges" while warning of the "heighten[ed] . . . potential for 'cronyism'" under it (Dodd et al. 2003).

The merit selection debate has long focused on judicial qualifications. More recently, stakeholders in the merit selection debate have also made claims about the connection between institutional reform and judicial diversity. Many proponents claim that insulating judicial selection decisions from political pressure increases the likelihood that members of historically underrepresented groups such as women and racial minorities will be chosen. One scholar claimed, for example, that "there is no question but that the merit selection system affords greater opportunities for women and minorities to find their way to the bench" (Krivosha 1987, 19). But for each assertion that "states using merit selection have a more diverse judiciary than states that don't" (Mah 1994), another suggests that "merit selection . . . has not helped diversify the state court judiciary in terms of race, ethnicity or gender" (Maute 2000, 1198).

Conflicting claims about the consequences of merit selection for issues such as judicial qualifications and diversity are empirical in nature (cf. Bonneau and Hall 2009). Nonetheless, much like the broader judicial selection and retention debates, positions on these questions are often driven more by prior normative commitments than empirical observation. To be sure, numerous empirical studies have examined whether merit selection is more or less likely to produce state supreme court justices with particular characteristics.[5] As informative as these studies are, however, many were undertaken when merit selection was in its infancy. Moreover, much of the existing literature relies on data from narrow time windows and small samples of states. In addition, few studies account for the method by which particular judges were selected. These limitations make it difficult to draw confident conclusions about the core question of whether merit selection produces different types of judges. Absent firm empirical evidence regarding the consequences of alternative institutional arrangements, we are left to speculate.

In this book, I use new data on more than 1,500 state supreme court justices seated from 1960 through 2014, along with extensive biographical information collected for these justices, to undertake the first large-scale empirical analysis of whether merit selection produces judges with characteristics that systematically differ from judges produced by other selection systems. The results have important implications for the core policy debate regarding whether merit selection "populate[s] the bench with individuals who are qualitatively different" than judges chosen under other selection systems (Caufield 2010, 766). Moreover, this project contributes to the broader debate concerning comparative institutional performance with respect to state judicial selection.

While the empirical results have normative implications, they are not employed here to advance an argument for or against any particular judicial selection mechanism. Although the outcomes analyzed here play a central role in contemporary policy debates over the efficacy of various judicial selection institutions, reasonable observers can disagree over how to weight their relative importance. Moreover, while the outcomes analyzed here are among the most referred to in contemporary judicial selection debates, they are certainly not the only relevant factors worth considering when determining which selection system to adopt. One prevalent argument against merit selection, for example, is that it is inconsistent with democratic values (e.g., Olszewski 2004; Schneider 2010; Uehlein and Wilderman 2002).[6] To the extent that some stakeholders consider this point dispositive, empirical evidence concerning institutional performance is likely to be of secondary importance. As discussed further in the Conclusion, debates over the "best" judicial selection system are particularly complex given little agreement about what selection systems are supposed to accomplish. Even if the debate cannot be resolved here, however, the results help inform the discussion and provide insight into the relationship between selection institutions and the characteristics of justices chosen to serve on state supreme courts.

Clarifying Merit Selection

The phrase "merit selection" regularly engenders conceptual confusion. Thus, I clarify what merit selection means at the outset. As an initial matter, merit selection should be distinguished from the "merit plan" or "Missouri plan." Although these three phrases are often used interchangeably, the former is conceptually distinct from the latter two. As noted previously, merit selection's core component is the use of a commission to winnow judicial candidates before elite appointment. Under the merit plan, judges are chosen through merit selection and retained through retention elections.[7] Consequently, merit selection is a necessary but not a sufficient condition for instituting the merit plan. Indeed, merit selection can be linked to any retention institution based on preferences concerning the trade-off between judicial independence and accountability.[8] Rhode Island, for example, combines merit selection with life tenure.[9] In 2015, Oregon legislators proposed amending the state's constitution to switch from nonpartisan elections for selection and retention to merit selection with merit-based reappointment by the nominating commission after a fixed term.[10] This variation illustrates the need for distinguishing debates over judicial selection and retention in the states (cf. Ware 2009, 751).[11]

Distinguishing merit selection from the merit plan is not the only complicating issue underlying empirical examinations of merit selection. Notwithstanding general agreement regarding merit selection's core feature, there seems to be disagreement over which states use merit selection to fill supreme court vacancies. Recent articles listing merit selection states, for example, have counts ranging from fifteen to twenty-eight.[12] Even scholars employing an indicator for merit selection states in quantitative analyses seem to differ over which states to include (see, e.g., Choi, Gulati, and Posner 2010; Kang and Shepherd 2011; McLeod 2012). That scholars appear to mean different things when referring to merit selection raises considerable concern about the inferences that can be drawn from the literature examining merit selection's consequences. Moreover, this classification issue fundamentally affects our ability to draw inferences about judicial selection institutions more generally: that there are differences in categorizing states using merit selection necessarily means there are differences in categorizing some of the states using alternative selection methods.

Merit selection categorization issues do not proceed merely from the tendency to conflate merit selection and the merit plan. Most contemporary merit selection lists correctly include every state that employs the merit plan. Differences arise over which states to include in addition to those operating under the merit plan. California seems to be the most common mistaken inclusion in merit selection lists. In California, a governor's supreme court nominee must be confirmed by the Commission on Judicial Appointments before taking office.[13] This institutional arrangement effectively inverts merit selection, affording the commission veto power over an otherwise unconstrained gubernatorial choice rather than constraining it ex ante. Other states are mistakenly excluded from merit selection lists, including Connecticut, Hawaii, New York, and Rhode Island. Each of these states uses a nominating commission to screen applicants for supreme court vacancies. Although it is not clear why these states are sometimes excluded, it may be because of their somewhat irregular institutional combinations of merit selection with retention mechanisms other than retention elections.

Voluntary merit selection systems are another source of confusion when attempting to list merit selection states. As opposed to states that enact merit selection through statute or constitutional amendment, voluntary merit selection systems are unilaterally devised and implemented by governors—often through executive order (Lowe 1971; Vandenberg 1983). As such, they can also be abolished through unilateral executive action. In fact, original-enacting or subsequently elected governors have abolished several merit selection systems initially established through unilateral gubernatorial action. The comparative institutional transiency inherent in voluntary merit selection systems complicates efforts to locate information about their presence and operation. Indeed, no comprehensive listing of these plans seems to be available. As a result, scholars tend to include some but not all of the known voluntary merit selection system states in their listings.

One additional factor complicates efforts to evaluate merit selection's consequences. Contrary to most institutions governing state judiciaries, merit selection is both a state-level and justice-level phenomenon. All supreme court justices serving contemporaneously within a state are presumed to be subject to the same retention institution, term limit, and mandatory retirement age.[14] But the same is not true with respect to judicial selection institutions. Currently, seven states employ merit selection for interim appointments to their supreme courts but not otherwise. This dual institutional arrangement exemplifies the broader phenomenon of mixed judicial selection systems, in which different institutional mechanisms are used to fill regular and interim vacancies. Notwithstanding these dual arrangements, scholars generally do not account for how particular state supreme court justices were seated when evaluating the consequences of different institutional design choices regarding judicial selection. Given that a substantial proportion of state supreme court justices obtain their seats through interim appointments (Holmes and Emrey 2006), it is important to account for the way that specific justices took the bench when evaluating comparative institutional performance regarding judicial selection.

Table 1.1 groups states that have employed commission-based judicial appointments for their supreme courts into four categories.[15] The first column lists states that have adopted merit selection for all their supreme court justices, distinguishing between those that have done so through statute or constitutional amendment (toward the top) and those that have done so through unilateral gubernatorial action (toward the bottom).[16] The third column lists states that have adopted merit selection for interim appointments, distinguishing between those that have done so through statute or constitutional amendment

TABLE 1.1 MERIT SELECTION SYSTEMS

All appointments	Adoption	Interim appointments	Adoption
Constitutional and statutory			
Alaska	1959	Idaho	1967
Arizona	1974	Kentucky	1975
Colorado	1966	Montana	1972
Connecticut	1986	Nevada	1976
Florida	1972	New Mexico	1988
Hawaii	1978	North Dakota	1976
Indiana	1970	Utah	1967–1985
Iowa	1962	West Virginia	2010
Kansas	1958		
Missouri	1940		
Nebraska	1962		
New York	1977		
Oklahoma	1967		
Rhode Island	1994		
South Dakota	1980		
Tennessee	1971–1974, 1994–2013		
Utah	1985		
Vermont	1967		
Wyoming	1972		
Voluntary			
Delaware	1977	Colorado	1964–1966
Maine	2011	Florida	1971–1972
Maryland	1970	Georgia	1972
Massachusetts	1975	Mississippi	1980–1991
New Hampshire	2000	Montana	1968–1972
New York	1975–1977	New Mexico	1952–1988
Tennessee	2013	North Carolina	2011–2012
		Ohio	1972–1974
		Pennsylvania	1973–1994
		South Dakota	1977–1980
		West Virginia	1981–2010
		Wisconsin	1983

(toward the top) and those that have done so through unilateral gubernatorial action (toward the bottom). The adoption columns denote the year each plan was adopted; years listed alone indicate that the plan was still in operation through 2014. Eighteen states employed nonvoluntary merit selection plans to choose all supreme court justices at the end of 2014, and another seven states employed nonvoluntary merit selection plans for interim appointments. At least six states employed voluntary merit selection plans at the end of 2014, with two others using them to fill only interim vacancies.

Merit selection's proponents regularly suggest that no state adopting merit selection subsequently switched to a different system (see, e.g., Finley 2003, 55; Phillips 2009, 93). This claim is sometimes made to demonstrate merit selection's success. Table 1.1 reveals two caveats to this claim. First, several states have abolished voluntary merit selection plans. Mississippi's "fleeting" (Case 1992, 26–29) experiment with voluntary merit selection, for example, spanned three gubernatorial administrations. More recently, North Carolina's experiment with voluntary merit selection lasted for even less time. Declaring, "There is no place for politics when it comes to choosing the state's most honored and influential legal servants," Democratic North Carolina governor Bev Perdue issued an executive order establishing voluntary merit selection in 2011 (Hardin 2011). One year later, and about one month before Republican governor-elect Pat McCrory assumed office, Governor Perdue issued another executive order "temporarily" suspending the commission in order to unilaterally fill a supreme court vacancy before leaving office (see Perdue 2012). Governor McCrory formally abolished the commission after taking office (see McCrory 2013).

The second caveat involves Tennessee's somewhat peculiar history with merit selection. Before November 2014, Tennessee's constitution provided that "judges of the Supreme Court shall be elected by the qualified voters of the state."[17] Notwithstanding this language, Tennessee enacted legislation in 1971 adopting merit selection for its appellate judges (see Fitzpatrick 2008). Although the statutory provision instituting merit selection for state supreme court justices was repealed in 1974, it was reimplemented by statute in 1994 and persisted into 2012 despite concerns about its constitutionality. In 2012, the state legislature allowed the law's sunset clause to take effect, and the nominating commission ceased operations in 2013. After cessation, Governor Bill Haslam created a voluntary merit selection plan by executive order. In 2014, voters approved a constitutional amendment giving the governor unilateral appointment authority, and the voluntary merit selection plan remained in place.

Ambiguity in the existing literature necessitates adopting a clear and objective decision rule regarding which states employ merit selection to choose state supreme court justices. In the empirical analyses presented in Chapters 3 through 5, I focus exclusively on nonvoluntary merit selection institutions. The primary difficulties with including voluntary merit selection systems are that their comparative institutional transiency can make it difficult to know which states have employed them, when they were functioning, and how they operated.[18] Where appropriate, however, I note how inferences about comparative institutional performance change when including known voluntary merit selection plans. This approach offers the benefits of transparency and replicability while allowing readers to draw their own conclusions about merit selection's consequences if there are conflicting results. Overall, however, the results are substantively similar regardless of whether voluntary merit selection plans are included with nonvoluntary plans.

Why Study Merit Selection?

The U.S. Supreme Court is easily the most publicly visible and researched court in the nation—perhaps the world. Nonetheless, state supreme courts are far more active and arguably have a greater aggregate policy impact. From 1995 through 2010, for example, state supreme courts decided over 16,000 percent more cases than the U.S. Supreme Court.[19] Furthermore, the average state supreme court decided about 30 percent more cases than the U.S. Supreme Court per year during this period. State supreme courts are often leaders in shaping public policy in areas such as education and civil liberties (Howard and Steigerwalt 2012). And state supreme court dockets cover nearly the entire range of public (e.g., constitutional and criminal) and private (e.g., contracts and torts) law (see Kritzer et al. 2007).[20] Although any particular state supreme court decision is unlikely to garner national attention, many are salient within states (e.g., Cann and Wilhelm 2011; Vining and Wilhelm 2011; Vining et al. 2010). Furthermore, in addition to enjoying the last word on most questions concerning state law, state supreme courts regularly decide important federal questions.[21] In short, "state supreme courts are powerful institutions with a dramatic impact upon the American political landscape" (Brace, Hall, and Langer 2001, 82).

The judicial decision-making literature offers another justification for taking judicial selection seriously. Scholars have long debated the determinants of judicial behavior (e.g., Epstein, Landes, and Posner 2013; Geyh 2011; Segal and Spaeth 2002), with alternative accounts emphasizing factors such as law, policy preferences, and institutional constraints. Although this complex debate shows no signs of imminent resolution, nearly everyone seems to agree that judges are not merely automatons uniformly disposing cases through a mechanical process that can be mastered only with years of specialized legal training.[22] At a minimum, appellate judges on courts of last resort occasionally resolve difficult legal questions on which reasonable minds can differ (see, e.g., Farber and Sherry 2008; Posner 2005; Zorn and Bowie 2010). This discretionary space in how important legal questions are resolved justifies paying careful attention to judicial selection decisions.

Understanding judicial selection also contributes to the developing mosaic of evidence regarding the consequences of institutional reform with respect to state judiciaries. Interstate institutional experimentation allows stakeholders to glean important insights about comparative institutional performance. With respect to state courts, for example, scholars have studied the impact of judicial selection and retention institutions on an array of political phenomena, including voting and elections (e.g., Bonneau and Cann 2015a, 2015b; Bonneau and Loepp 2014; Melinda Gann Hall 2007, 2015; Kritzer 2015), campaign spending (e.g., Bonneau 2004, 2005, 2007; Hall and Bonneau 2008), separate opinion writing (e.g., Boyea 2007, 2010; Brace and Hall 1990, 1993), tenure on the bench (e.g., Boyea 2010; Melinda Gann Hall 2001b, 2013), perceptions of institutional legitimacy (e.g., Benesh 2006; Cann and Yates 2007; Gibson 2012), judicial performance (e.g., Cann 2006; Goelzhauser 2012; Goelzhauser and Cann 2014; M. Nelson 2013), and judicial decision making (e.g., Brace and Boyea 2008; Canes-Wrone, Clark, and Kelly 2014; Melinda Gann Hall 1992).[23] Thoroughly examining merit selection's comparative institutional performance necessarily dictates measuring the impact of other judicial selection systems. As a result, the study of merit selection is effectively a broader inquiry into the consequences of institutional reform in the area of state judicial selection.

Debates over institutional design choices concerning state judicial selection and retention also permeate contemporary political discourse. For example, recent U.S. Supreme Court decisions such as *Republican Party of Minnesota v. White* (2002), *Caperton v. A. T. Massey Coal Co.* (2009), and *Williams-Yulee v. The Florida Bar* (2015) helped bring debates concerning state judicial selection and retention into sharp national focus.[24] And merit selection in particular has been at the forefront of the contemporary debate over state judicial selection. Former U.S. Supreme Court justice Sandra Day O'Connor, for example, has devoted a considerable portion of her postretirement public life to advocating for merit selection.[25] Moreover, numerous states are currently considering whether to adopt, expand, limit, modify, or abolish merit selection for some or all of their judges. From 2009 through 2014, legislators in thirty states introduced a total of 390 bills involving merit selection.[26] In comparison, legislators in twenty-two states introduced a total of 136 bills that involved judicial selection institutions other than merit selection during the same period.[27]

The merit selection debate is also quickly expanding beyond the American states. There have been numerous discussions, for example, about commission-based judicial selection at the federal level (see, e.g., Sharon and Pettibone 1987; C. Smith 1987; Winters 1972). Moreover, other countries are beginning to experiment with commission-based judicial selection (see, e.g., J. Bell 2003; Evans and Williams 2008; Maute 2007). In 2006, the British Parliament abolished the position of lord chancellor, which historically controlled many judicial selection decisions, and instituted the Judicial Appointments Commission.[28] The new commission ostensibly sorts candidates on the basis of merit for judicial offices in England and Wales and some courts with jurisdiction over Northern Ireland and Scotland. After selecting a candidate, the commission forwards the name to the relevant appointing authority, who can accept the nomination or return it for another with written justification accompanying the rejection.[29] Northern Ireland's Judicial Appointments Commission and Scotland's Judicial Appointments Board operate similarly to the British commission in their respective countries.[30] Most recently, India is on the verge of implementing constitutional reform to establish a National Judicial Appointments Commission to select judges.[31]

Overview of the Chapters

How did merit selection originate? The institutional framework governing federal judicial selection has been fairly stable since the U.S. Constitution's ratification in 1789. The state level, however, has had considerable experimentation with judicial selection institutions since the first Revolutionary-era constitutions were adopted. Although these Revolutionary-era constitutions built on English and colonial judicial selection models using unilateral appointment, states soon began experimenting with elections. After a long period of experimentation and gradual institutional change, dissatisfaction with predominant selection methods led to the development of variations on what is now commonly called merit selection during the early part of the nineteenth century. Chapter 2 traces merit selection's rise by emphasizing the gradual institutional evolution and contemporary political shocks that motivated consideration of commission-based judicial selection reform.

The next three chapters analyze the relationship between judicial selection institutions and various outcomes of interest using new data on state supreme court seatings from 1960 through 2014. In Chapter 3, I analyze whether certain judicial selection institutions favor candidates with different types of professional experience. This issue has gained importance with recent political and scholarly reflection on the consequences of experiential diversity for collegial courts and from growing understanding of how professional experiences inform judicial decision making. Moreover, professional experience provides the lens through which commentators have addressed the question of whether merit selection enhances or mitigates the importance of political connections in judicial selection decisions. Using new employment categories and extensive original data on the professional experiences possessed by state supreme court justices seated during the sample period, the results suggest there is little difference in the types of experiences favored across selection systems.

For decades, merit selection's proponents and critics have made bold claims about the system's performance in yielding better-qualified judges. Chapter 4 addresses this core question in the debate. Unfortunately, the little empirical evidence that exists on this question does not lend itself to confident conclusions about the relationship between judicial selection systems and qualifications. Using an array of measures to capture judicial qualifications, the results presented in Chapter 4 add nuance to our understanding of the relationship between selection systems and qualifications while generally supporting the position that there are few systematic differences. Indeed, selection systems perform similarly with respect to sorting on various measures of judicial experience. Although there are some differences across selection institutions in terms of educational quality and performance, no system enjoys a systematic advantage over the others.

While the debate over how to design judicial selection institutions has long focused on qualifications, recent decades have seen burgeoning interest in the relationship between selection institutions and judicial diversification with respect to women and racial minorities. This issue has become particularly salient in debates over merit selection, with proponents arguing that their favored system increases judicial diversity by reducing the importance of political connections and critics arguing that at best it has no effect and at worst a deleterious one on diversity. After tracing the development of political interest in judicial diversity and the consequences of selection institutions for realizing this goal, Chapter 5 analyzes the relationship between judicial selection systems and the seating of women and racial minorities on state supreme courts. The results suggest that appointment systems outperform merit selection and elections in some categories and that merit selection outperforms elections in others.

Chapter 6 concludes by summarizing the results, discussing normative implications, and highlighting important issues for future research. Ultimately, the results presented throughout this book have important normative implications that must be considered in combination with a flourishing literature on the consequences of institutional design choices concerning state judicial selection and retention. Determining which judicial selection system is "best" may be a complicated task, but at a minimum it is one that requires piecing together the mosaic of research on state courts, considering normative questions involving issues such as the trade-off between accountability and independence, determining how to weight the available information, and updating our prior beliefs as new information becomes available. Even within the scope of this study, no single selection system emerges as "best" relative to the others. Rather, it seems that certain selection systems outperform others in certain areas but mostly perform similarly. While this may not be the message that any system's staunchest supporters or critics would hope for, it is consistent with the complexity of the broader debate and should nonetheless help inform policy discussions.

2 | MERIT SELECTION'S RISE

W hat are merit selection's origins? It is a relatively new institutional innovation in America's long-running effort to find the optimal method for choosing judges. Formal institutions such as judicial selection procedures are often highly resistant to change. Institutional stickiness may be from factors such as popular acquiescence, support from powerful stakeholders, and the high transaction costs associated with reform. Although federal judicial selection institutions have essentially remained stable since the U.S. Constitution's ratification in 1789, the states have experimented with institutional frameworks governing judicial selection since the first Revolutionary-era constitutions were adopted. In short, "state judicial selection does not occur in a political vacuum" (Tarr 2003, 1453). This chapter traces merit selection's rise by focusing on state-led institutional experimentation and important contemporary political shocks that motivated reform efforts.

Historical Origins

In the colonial era, English judges were selected by the lord chancellor on behalf of the Crown.[1] Under the original colonial charters, lord proprietors were often invested with unilateral authority to appoint judges and other public officials. For example, the 1681 Charter for the Province of Pennsylvania declared that the Crown did "give and grant unto the said William Penn, and his heires, and to his and their Deputies and Lieutenants, full power and authoritie to appoint and establish any Judges and Justices, Magistrates and Officers whatsoever, for what Causes soever for the probates of wills, and for the granting of Administrations within the precincts aforesaid and with what Power soever, and in such forme as to the said William Penn or his heires shall seeme most convenient."[2] In practice, appointment authority was often vested in royal governors, who in turn used the positions as patronage (Volcansek and Lafon 1988). In accordance with English practice and the grant of colonial charters, heredity played an important role in determining who would fill judicial vacancies. One historical anecdote from 1752, for example, concerns a person who "without previous training" had been "appointed Judge of Probate and Justice of the Common Pleas for the County of Suffolk, in place of an uncle, just dead" (Hosmer 1896, 46, 37). As the colonial courts were "extremely important legal and social institutions" (G. E. White 2012, 81), Revolutionary-era reformers paid close attention to matters of institutional design.

In May 1776, the Second Continental Congress resolved that because "no Government sufficient to the exigencies of their affairs has been hitherto established," the colonies should "adopt such Government as shall, in the opinion of the Representatives of the People, best conduce to the happiness and safety of their constituents in particular and America in general."[3] Less than two months later the same congress unanimously passed the Declaration of Independence, which included among its objections to England's King George III that "He has made Judges dependent on his Will alone, for the tenure of their offices, and the amount and payment of their salaries."[4] These opening salvos triggered the beginning of America's experiment with self-governance and set the ongoing debate over judicial selection in motion.

By the end of 1776, many states had already heeded the Second Continental Congress's call to adopt new constitutions, and others followed soon thereafter. These state constitutions played a fundamental role in American constitutional development (see, e.g., Dinan 2006;

Tarr 1998; Zackin 2013). Indeed, "the structure and form of the new federal government of 1787 was the direct product of what had taken place in the making of the state governments during the [Revolutionary era]" (G. Wood 1993, 911). Each of the states that ratified constitutions before the U.S. Constitution's adoption chose some form of appointment to govern the selection of judges to their highest courts. Although institutional arrangements differed across states, all dispersed authority among multiple officials. Five states delegated judicial selection authority to their legislatures, four divided authority between some variation of a governor and council, and one divided authority between the executive and legislative branches.[5] While Georgia is typically credited as the first to institute elections for lower court judges in 1812, Vermont's 1777 constitution provided for "county elections" at which "freemen in each county respectively, shall have the liberty of choosing the judges of inferior court of common pleas, sheriff', justices of the peace, and judges of probates, commissioned by the Governor and Council, during good behavior, removable by the General Assembly upon proof of mal-administration."[6]

Adoption of the Articles of Confederation in 1781 formally initiated the federal government's constitutional experiment. Although the Articles of Confederation did not establish a federal judiciary, it did afford Congress the "sole and exclusive right and power of . . . appointing courts for the trial of piracies and felonies commited [sic] on the high seas and establishing courts for receiving and determining finally appeals in all cases of captures, provided that no member of Congress shall be appointed a judge of any of the said courts."[7] As with early state constitutions, this preliminary foray into federal judicial selection reflected contemporary concern with vesting too much unilateral appointment authority.

English practice and early American constitutional development informed the way delegates to the Constitutional Convention of 1787 approached judicial selection.[8] The Virginia Plan, which helped guide deliberation over a number of institutional design choices, proposed that federal judges be appointed by the legislature.[9] Subsequently, James Wilson spoke in favor of presidential appointment, while James Madison proposed Senate appointment (Ziskind 1969, 149). Shortly after the Virginia Plan was revised to provide for Senate appointment as favored by Madison, William Patterson introduced the New Jersey Plan, calling for executive appointment. With the convention moving toward Madison's plan, Nathaniel Gorham proposed presidential appointment with the Senate's advice and consent (Gauch 1989, 341).[10] Although delegates voted down Gorham's proposal, Madison suggested two variations: one calling for at least one-third of the Senate's support, the other suggesting a switch in the default rule to absence of Senate objection (A. White 2005, 115–116). After the Committee on Compromise subsequently debated and later revived Gorham's proposal, the convention ultimately approved what would become the Appointments Clause granting the president nominating authority subject to the Senate's "advise and consent."[11] Gouverneur Morris summarized the justification for this compromise position when he noted that "as the President was to nominate, there would be responsibility, and as the Senate was to concur, there would be security" (Farrand 1966, 539).

The convention's delegates do not seem to have seriously considered judicial elections (Volcansek and Lafon 1988, 30). Moreover, little effort has been expended pursuing major reform to judicial selection institutions at the federal level since the U.S. Constitution's ratification in 1789.[12] This political acquiescence may be attributed to a variety factors, including perception that the nomination and consent process works well enough and resignation to supermajority requirements governing constitutional amendment that substantially increase the transaction costs associated with institutional reform. The status quo prevailed in the states for many years as well. After the original thirteen states adopted various forms of judicial appointment, the next sixteen to enter the Union—beginning with Vermont in 1791 and ending with Iowa in 1846—provided for either executive or legislative appointment. However, this period of institutional stability did not last.

After Vermont's experiment with judicial elections for certain lower court judges ended with its 1786 constitution, Georgia became the next state to adopt judicial elections in 1812. These elections were limited to inferior courts, which were a type of trial court with limited jurisdiction.[13] In 1832, Mississippi's newly ratified constitution made it the first state to elect all its judges. Committed to regular elections as an accountability mechanism, Jacksonian Democrats won a hard-fought political battle to initiate this institutional change. Following Mississippi's switch, however, five more states entered the Union providing for judicial selection through legislative or executive appointment, and no other state changed its system during the next fifteen years.

New York triggered a large-scale shift to partisan elections after adopting the reform in its 1846 constitution following a long history with gubernatorial appointment. New York is said to have "stumbled into judicial elections almost by accident" because reform pressures were not a driving force behind constitutional revision efforts and were probably not strong enough to secure change absent a convention (Shugerman 2010, 1084). Once the state committed to a constitutional convention, however, the push for judicial elections received broad support because of concerns about checking increased legislative power and curtailing politically motivated appointments (Shugerman 2010). Following New York's switch, the next seventeen states to enter the Union—beginning with Wisconsin in 1848 and ending with Oklahoma in 1906—all adopted partisan elections. Furthermore, during this same period, eighteen states that had previously adopted legislative or executive appointment switched to partisan elections.

Scholars disagree about why judicial elections suddenly gained popularity. New York's adoption might have conferred a measure of credibility to the institution that was lacking after Mississippi's switch given the latter's relatively weak standing as a policy leader (Aumann 1940). A delegate to New York's 1846 convention expressed a contemporary sentiment when he opposed judicial elections by complaining that "in no where but the assassin, repudiating slave state of Mississippi" were judges elected (Bishop and Attree 1846, 792). More generally, Jacksonian democracy is often credited as a catalyst in the diffusion of judicial elections (e.g., Sturm 1982). As one scholar summarizes Jacksonian democracy's influence on electoral reform during this period, "The ballot had been short in the early days of the Republic, but later it was decided that not only the councilmen should be directly elected by the people, but also the Mayor, the Coroner, the dog-catcher, and a host of others" (Hermens 1940, 392). With respect to the adoption of judicial elections during this time, one scholar suggests that "the movement was based on emotion rather than on a deliberate evaluation of experience under the appointive system" (Hurst 1950, 140).

Recent historical treatments offer a more complex understanding of why judicial elections became more popular during this period.[14] By one account, politically moderate lawyers and judges who believed that elections enhanced judicial power and prestige led the push for reform (K. Hall 1983, 1984). This explanation rests in part on the view that members of the legal community increasingly considered appointed judges to be of lower quality based on the perception that they catered to political pressure too readily. Moreover, lawyers and judges are said to have believed that elections would enhance judicial power by lending credibility to the exercise of judicial review. Contrary to the contention that judicial elections were intended to increase judicial power, an alternative perspective suggests that moving away from appointments was part of a more general trend toward diminishing government power and minimizing agency loss by transferring judicial selection authority from politicians to the public (N. Nelson 1993). Yet another perspective highlights the importance of contemporary state constitutional conventions to deal with economic crises, rein in legislative power, and address swelling sentiment that elections would help strengthen judicial review and protect individual rights and liberties from government encroachment (Shugerman 2010).

Empirical studies supplement these narratives with more specific observations. One study, for example, identifies several state-level factors influencing the adoption of partisan judicial elections during this period (Hanssen 2004). As suggested by various historical accounts, states holding constitutional conventions at the time (typically for reasons unrelated to judicial selection) were substantially more likely to adopt judicial elections. This is understandable in light of the high transaction costs otherwise associated with constitutional reform. Furthermore, states with long-entrenched incumbents were less likely to adopt judicial elections. This result follows from the more general principle that governing parties with firm control of political institutions are likely to favor the status quo. Empirical results also suggest that time since joining the Union, Democratic political control, and population size are positively associated with the probability of states switching from appointment to election during this period.

Popular perception that political elites and party bosses exerted undue influence over elections soon dampened enthusiasm for this institutional reform. In New York, for example, the Tammany Hall political machine controlled nominations and influenced elections to ensure its judges could dole out patronage, enforce corrupt political bargains, and oversee election rigging (see, e.g., Lerner 2007; G. Myers 1917; Shortell 2010). Tammany Hall leader William "Boss" Tweed often selected judges personally rather than delegating the task to local leaders, and the machine's influence over the judiciary was so extensive and important to regime maintenance that its eventual erosion was considered "instrumental in [Tweed's] ultimate downfall from power" (Shortell 2010, 220). Less than twenty-five years after New York switched from appointment to election, the political intrigue that accompanied elections led to a popular vote on a referendum to bring back judicial appointments in 1873 (Lerner 2007). Although the New York referendum failed, other states confronting similar issues with judicial elections switched to judicial appointments around this time (Winters 1966).

Frustration with partisan judicial elections reached a tipping point in the early twentieth century. Many observers believed that political parties controlled judicial elections and used them to place party faithful on the bench. One delegate to the Ohio Constitutional Convention of 1912 complained, for example, that "the election of judges places the power of their selection on political managers and bosses, who are self-selected and chosen and who are not responsible to any tribunal whatever for the exercise of their power" (*Proceedings and Debates* 1912, 1052). The sentiment that political parties dominated judicial elections helped propel the Progressive reform movement around the turn of the twentieth century. Nonpartisan elections for a variety of public offices were a key part of the bundle of institutional reforms designed to diminish the influence of political parties and return power to the people (Schaffner, Streb, and Wright 2001). On a nonpartisan ballot, candidate names are displayed without corresponding party labels. As a result, nonpartisan ballots theoretically require voters to make decisions without relying on political party as a heuristic.

From 1911 through 1916, one state switched its judicial selection mechanism from appointment to nonpartisan election and nine states switched from partisan to nonpartisan election. In addition, Arizona joined the Union in 1912 having adopted nonpartisan election. Two states chose partisan election during this period, and none chose appointment. Although other states continued adopting nonpartisan judicial elections in the ensuing decades, many observers considered the reform an almost immediate failure in its goals to diminish political influence over judicial selection decisions, improve the quality of the bench, and strengthen citizen participation (Shugerman 2012, 170). In 1913, the year his presidential term ended and eight years before becoming chief justice of the U.S. Supreme Court, William Howard Taft delivered a scathing address to the American Bar Association (ABA) condemning the rise of judicial elections. According to Taft, nonpartisan elections were even "less satisfactory" than partisan elections because of the lack of "anything . . . to guide the voter" in making an informed decision. Taft further lamented that "men who were not candidates were nominated for the Bench, but now in no case can the office seek the man" as a result of judges having to campaign vigorously in order to ensure electability in an environment where citizens did not have access to a meaningful decision heuristic (Taft 1913, 422).[15]

The Movement Begins

Dissatisfaction with existing judicial selection institutions eventually led to merit selection's rise. The story of merit selection's intellectual origins often begins with Roscoe Pound's 1906 address to the ABA. Pound was a professor at Harvard Law School at the time and later became one of the nation's most influential legal scholars. Pound's address considered various "causes of popular dissatisfaction with the administration of justice." Although judicial elections were not Pound's primary emphasis, one of his concluding points suggested that "putting courts into politics and compelling judges to become politicians in many jurisdictions has almost destroyed the traditional respect for the bench" (Pound 1906, 450). Although others made similar arguments at the time, Pound went on to cofound the American Judicature Society in 1913. While the American Judicature Society emphasized questions concerning judicial administration more generally, it also became a prominent advocacy group in the campaign for merit selection and remained so until its dissolution in 2014.[16]

Early merit selection plans began circulating shortly after Pound's address to the ABA. Like Pound, many commentators increasingly disliked judicial elections and thus favored institutional reform, which was consistent with Progressive Era sentiment more generally. At an influential Georgia Bar Association meeting in 1909, for example, one symposium participant called popular elections "the worst [selection method] that has ever been inflicted on the people" and urged that courts "be as far removed from popular vote and influence as possible" (G. Owens 1909, 212–213). Another participant suggested that "the office of Judge ought to be gotten just as far away from the people as it is possible to carry it" (Pope 1909, 220). Building on prevailing sentiment, a symposium participant named John T. Norris proposed "the enactment of a statute requiring the Governor of the State to send to the State Senate . . . the names of three practitioners . . . from which three names, the Senate shall elect a Judge" for trial court vacancies (1909, 218). Hewlett Hall, another participant, proposed that trial court judges "should be nominated by the Supreme Court, appointed by the Governor and confirmed by the Senate" (1909, 226). The supreme court nomination provision reflected a growing sense that sitting judges were well situated to evaluate prospective judges, while executive and legislative involvement provided a dual check against political intrigue.

Albert Kales, another of the American Judicature Society's early members, is often credited with proposing the first merit selection plan.[17] After calling it a "fundamental error" to classify appointment and election as different judicial selection systems in practice, Kales wrote:

> There is, speaking generally, only one method of selecting judges, and that is by appointment. There are, of course, different kinds of appointment, . . . but except perhaps in the most primitive frontier communities, there is no such thing as the selection of judges by the people. In metropolitan districts I venture to say that such a method of selection not only does not exist, but cannot by any possibility exist. It is one of our most

> absurd bits of political hypocrisy that we actually talk and act
> as if our judges were elected by the people whenever the method
> of selection is, in form, by popular election. (1914a, 32)

This position followed from a common belief among contemporary reformers that political parties controlled judicial selection outcomes regardless of the institutional mechanism employed and that, in any event, citizens were too ignorant of the judiciary to make informed decisions. If all judges were to be appointed in practice regardless of the selection mechanism employed in principle, Kales encouraged reformers to reconsider the optimal appointment method.

Kales argued that "the least objectionable method of appointment and the one which promises the most, is that of vesting the appointing power in an elective chief justice who is given large powers over and responsibility for the way in which the court operates" (1914a, 42). As with Hewlett Hall's proposal in Georgia, Kales's suggestion to vest the chief justice with appointment authority stemmed from a belief that those who occupied this position were uniquely qualified to evaluate prospective judges. As a check on the chief justice's authority, Kales proposed that a "judicial council" comprising other state judges be vested with authority to formulate a list of judicial candidates from which the chief justice would be required to select "on the occasion of every other appointment at least" (1914b, 250).

The possibility of using judges to screen candidates gained momentum in the years following Kales's proposal. A Louisiana Bar Association plan proposed in advance of a state constitutional convention in 1921, for example, gave judges a pivotal role in nominations. For trial and appellate judges, the proposal provided that any "vacancy shall be filled by appointment by the Governor, by and with the consent of the Senate, from a list alphabetically arranged of not less than three or more than five eligibles certified to him by a majority of the Supreme Judicial Council" (Louisiana Bar Association 1920, 10). For supreme court vacancies, the remaining justices would construct the list of candidates to be delivered to the governor.[18] The Louisiana Bar Association's defense of this "novel" (12) design neatly summarized the growing contemporary sentiment that more traditional judicial selection methods worked poorly in practice:

In our view, if either of these [appointive or elective] systems could be made to work in consonance with the theories of their respective advocates, either would insure a satisfactory judiciary. If political expediency, personal popularity and political intrigue were disregarded, and the people really exercised an intelligent, independent choice, based only upon judicial fitness of the candidates, then there could be no objection to the elective system. If, on the other hand, we could be sure that the Governor would cease to regard judicial office as a personal gift or reward to the faithful, if the judges so appointed felt less need to curry favor with the immediate appointing power than with the people, if absolute independence of popular opinion did not frequently engender irresponsibility and arbitrariness, appointive judges would be more satisfactory. But in cold practice, in present day conditions, political, social or economic, neither system works true to theory. (19–20)

In delegating screening authority to judges, the Louisiana Bar Association emphatically echoed Kales, lauding the "body of men presumably themselves chosen, from throughout the States, for fitness of character and mind, occupying the highest judicial positions in the State, of mature age, free from the exigencies of political necessity through tenure for good behavior, ocupying [sic] positions bringing them into daily contact with the class from which judges must be chosen, and thus best qualified to choose and, presumably, barring inevitable human frailties, desirous of obtaining the best qualified men to occupy positions with them on the bench" (20). Although the Louisiana Bar Association's plan was not adopted, the proposal and supporting arguments were indicative of a growing momentum for reform.

Illinois nearly became the first state to adopt merit selection in 1922 with a variation of Kales's proposal to enlist judges in the selection process. At the time, Cook County (encompassing Chicago) courts were inefficient and fraught with corruption. Public officials were thought to control the county's judicial elections. One contemporary commentator, and past president of the Chicago Bar Association, complained that "there has been no real election of Circuit or Superior Court judges in Cook County since 1921, when the Republican party under the domination of [Chicago Mayor] William Hale Thompson and [Cook County Circuit Judge] Robert E. Crowe attempted to raid the bench, displace judges who were in their disfavor, and elect others whom they had selected" (Gardner, Fisher, and Martin 1936–1937, 894). To help remedy Cook County's problems, delegates to the Illinois Constitutional Convention, which met from 1920 to 1922, proposed consolidating Cook County's courts into a single entity and resolved that "the governor shall fill any vacancy in that court by appointment from a list containing the names of not less than four eligible persons for each vacancy, nominated by a majority of the supreme court, not more than one-half of such persons to be affiliated with the same political party" (*Journal of the Constitutional Convention* 1922, 797). Voters eventually rejected the proposed constitution, however, and the status quo prevailed in Cook County (Dodd 1923).

Noted English scholar Harold Laski's proposal that nonjudges be included on candidate review committees represented the next evolutionary step in merit selection's rise. Although perhaps best known for his correspondence with U.S. Supreme Court justice Oliver Wendell Holmes, Laski contributed to the ongoing debate over judicial selection with an influential article published by the *Michigan Law Review* in 1926. In that article, Laski claimed that "for the election of judges by popular vote there is nothing to be said," suggesting that people "with rare exceptions . . . merely vote for the colour they happen to prefer" (1926, 531). After ruling out alternatives, Laski concluded that "the nomination of the judges by the executive is the only feasible system of appointment." Nonetheless, Laski was concerned by the executive's natural inclination toward politically motivated appointments and thus suggested that "there be some advisory body whom the executive would consult about appointments" (538). Laski proposed similar systems for checking executive power over judicial nominations specific to England, the U.S. government, and the states. With respect to the states, Laski proposed that the "Governor would be assisted by a committee of the judges of the state supreme court, together with the state Attorney-General and the President of the State Bar Association" (539).

Commission-based judicial selection plans grew in popularity heading into the 1930s. Although the determinants of this momentum are difficult to isolate, the leading scholarly treatment suggests that "the three most important factors in merit's spread were first, business interests driving the campaign for merit reforms; second, urban leaders supporting merit reform; and third, the ability for these interests and leaders to win voters and broaden their coalitions" (Shugerman 2012, 179). Bar associations were among the most important constituents advocating for judicial selection reform during this time (McCormick 1935). A survey of state and local bar associations published in 1934 concluded that "lawyers in states where the judges are appointed by the governor or chosen by the legislature are strongly opposed to any change in the existing system, while the profession in those jurisdictions where the judges are elected is unsatisfied with present methods and wants something else" (Shafroth 1934, 529). Although the survey revealed that "little has been done toward adopting improved methods" (529), members of the bar who favored reform expressed support for a plan that would incorporate an "independent body" into the selection process (531).

Early Adoptions

After decades of slow intellectual evolution, California became the first state to adopt a variation of a commission-based judicial selection plan in 1934 when voters considered two plans. The California State Bar Association's judicial selection plan called for gubernatorial appointment from a list generated by a commission consisting of the chief justice of the California Supreme Court, the presiding judge of the district court of appeal overseeing the district with the vacancy, and the state senator who represented that area. After being introduced in the California State Assembly, the plan was amended and limited to counties with a population greater than 1.5 million—effectively making it applicable only to Los Angeles County (M. Smith 1951). An informational document provided by the state to voters included a passage from supporters contending that the plan would "enable the selection of better judges and take them out of politics"; the opposition argument in the document called the proposal "class legislation" that was "devoid" of any element designed to further "the elimination of politics" from judicial selection (F. Wood 1934, 21, 22). Voters ultimately rejected the proposed amendment despite legislative approval, vigorous backing from the state bar, and a broad coalition of support from other organized interests.

Developed by the California Committee on Better Administration of Law, the second proposed plan inverted merit selection's core structure. The committee, which included Alameda County district attorney and later chief justice of the U.S. Supreme Court Earl Warren, aimed to produce legislation that would "curb crime in California" (M. Smith 1951, 579–580).[19] The committee generated a series of proposals in addition to its judicial selection plan, including efforts to centralize law enforcement activities under one administrative umbrella, loosen procedural restrictions on judges overseeing criminal trials, and reform the plea bargaining process (Shugerman 2012). Although Warren and other committee members preferred instituting a judicial selection plan of gubernatorial appointment with life tenure, this option was considered a political nonstarter (M. Smith 1951). Instead, the committee eventually proposed that the governor appoint appellate judges subject to confirmation by a commission consisting of the chief justice of the California Supreme Court, attorney general, and presiding judge of the district court of appeal where the vacancy occurred. The committee also proposed allowing counties to approve a similar selection framework for local judges. An argument for the proposal included in the document delivered to voters read in part, "One of the chief obstacles to the proper administration of justice in California today is the fact that our judicial offices have become prizes to be fought for in the political arena, rather than positions of trust and confidence" (F. Wood 1934, 8). Unlike the California Bar Association's plan, the official guide did not include a counterargument and voters approved the measure.

Other merit selection plans quickly materialized following California's adoption of an inverted version in 1934. In 1937, for example, the Chicago Bar Association proposed an amendment to the Illinois Constitution calling for Cook County judges to be nominated by the governor from a list of at least five candidates approved by a bipartisan commission appointed by the local appellate court, with members prohibited from holding any public or political party office.[20] One Illinois judge criticized the plan as a "naive proposal for taking judges out of politics" that left them "six times removed from the people" (Fisher 1937, 903).[21] And after rejecting a proposal to switch from partisan to nonpartisan elections in 1934, Michigan voters rejected a statewide merit selection plan in 1938 (Wheat and Hurwitz 2013). Although the Michigan plan enjoyed support from state and local bar associations, opposition from the 1934 proposal's backers, "which included influential Wayne County [encompassing Detroit] judges, as well as the Detroit Chapter of the National Lawyers Guild, unions, a coalition of teachers and educators, one of the major Detroit newspapers and a local radio station with state broadcasting capabilities," proved too much to overcome (183).

By 1937, just three years after noting that "little has been done toward adopting improved [judicial selection] methods" (Shafroth 1934, 529), the ABA reported that over half the states with elected judiciaries were preparing commission-based reform proposals or had taken steps toward reform ("Report" 1937). In addition, the ABA adopted a resolution promoting merit selection for state judges. The resolution, offered as "the most acceptable substitute available for direct election of judges," called for "the filling of vacancies by appointment by the executive or other elective official or officials, but from a list named by another agency, composed in part of high judicial officers and in part of other citizens, selected for the purpose, who hold no other public office" (J. Wood 1937, 105). The chairman of the ABA's Committee on Judicial Selection and Tenure, John Perry Wood, subsequently lamented that "unless the bar and public realize that the administration of justice is sick, and are willing to set about a thorough-going cure, it [would be] better to wait until the need is more obvious or our courage stronger" to move ahead with reform, adding that "from all reports, the administration of justice in most of the elective states, and, particularly, in large cities, is sick enough" (J. Wood 1938, 541).

Although other states were considering merit selection plans for state supreme court justices, Missouri became the first to enact such a plan in 1940. The Missouri Plan was modeled after the ABA's proposal. Officially dubbed the "Nonpartisan Selection of Judges Court Plan" and put to voters as an initiative, the proposal called for gubernatorial appointment of appellate judges from a list of candidates supplied by a commission consisting of a Missouri Supreme Court justice, three lawyers, and three lay members—all of whom were to be appointed by the governor and could not be public office holders or party officials. The measure also applied to trial court judges in the city of St. Louis and Jackson County (encompassing Kansas City).[22] In addition, it called for judges to be retained via a noncontestable election with voters simply indicating whether the candidate should remain in office. Although the initiative's components had been previously proposed and discussed elsewhere, it subsequently became known as the Missouri Plan.

Several factors propelled Missouri's adoption of commission-based judicial selection reform. As an initial matter, proponents were well organized and highly successful in connecting reform justifications to the contemporary political environment. Various Missouri bar associations circled around different reform proposals before the Missouri Institute for the Administration of Justice formed to consolidate efforts under a single umbrella (Kirkendall 1986, 220). As a result of political resistance to the Missouri Plan, the institute leveraged its formidable statewide presence to gain ballot access by securing a sufficient number of signatures across congressional districts (Dunne 1993, 125). Moreover, an impressive coalition of stakeholders that included "business, elements of organized labor, women's groups, religious and educational organizations, and metropolitan newspapers" combined to thwart "the charge that the Plan was merely the creature of the Bar" (Watson and Downing 1969, 11). In addition, like California but unlike several states where reform efforts had failed, organizers strategically framed the proposal as a way to mitigate crime and political corruption (Shugerman 2010).

The political corruption connection proved to be a particularly effective catapult in Missouri, where machine politics notoriously reigned. Boss Tom Pendergast controlled Kansas City politics and exercised considerable influence at the state level with "his mastery of machine politics [and] his reputation and that of his organization for fostering corruption and flaunting law and order" (Larsen and Hulston 1997, xi). In a memorandum explaining the events surrounding Pendergast's conviction for tax evasion, federal district court judge Merrill Otis noted that "he who would be governor, he who would be senator, he who would be judge, and he who was content to be only a keeper of the pound" were required to obtain Pendergast's approval (*United States v. Pendergast* 1939, 602). Circumstances were similar in St. Louis, where party officials had recently created a scandal by securing a trial court judgeship for a full-time pharmacist whose eight years of bar membership included "fil[ing] nine suits, consisting of eight divorces and one annulment" (Bundschu 1948, 63). As a result of growing concern with political corruption, voters approved the Missouri Plan by a sizable margin (Blackmar 2007).

But the initiative's opponents did not readily concede defeat. Assuming "the people had merely made a mistake" (Bundschu 1948, 60), state legislators immediately moved to repeal the Missouri Plan. The newly organized opposition "attacked the Plan as a device of the press, insurance companies, and railroads to control the bench" and succeeded in getting a proposed repeal amendment on the ballot in 1942 (Watson and Downing 1969, 11). The absence of up-ticket presidential or gubernatorial races depressed overall turnout in 1942 compared to 1940, and voters defeated the repeal measure by a larger margin than the one that carried the first contest. A subsequent attempt to repeal the plan in the early 1940s during a state constitutional convention was scuttled when organizers abandoned the effort to ensure the new constitution's ratification (Blackmar 2007, 203).

Expansion

Merit selection remained dormant at the state level for nearly two decades following Missouri's hard-fought adoption.[23] The Alaska Constitution approved by voters in 1956 called for the gubernatorial appointment of judges from a commission-generated list. Delegates to the Alaska Constitutional Convention responsible for proposing the plan had been favorably impressed by Missouri's experience.[24] Moreover, Alaskans hoped their adoption of the plan would signal the state's commitment to maintaining a high-quality judiciary in an effort to secure support for admission to the Union (Shugerman 2012, 224–226). Although the constitution did not go into effect until Alaska obtained statehood in 1959, its consideration and approval demonstrated that the institutional arrangement remained a plausible alternative to then-dominant judicial selection methods.

Before Alaska joined the Union, Kansas officially became the second state to adopt merit selection for its highest court in 1958. Like Alaska, Kansas had been influenced by Missouri's experience with merit selection (Shugerman 2012). Efforts to establish merit selection in 1953 and 1955 failed to make it out of the Kansas legislature (Jackson 2000). In 1957, however, a scandal precipitated the switch to merit selection (see, e.g., Sanders 1995, 577–578; Ware 2008). The story begins with Republican governor Fred Hall losing his reelection bid in a primary, and Democrat George Docking ultimately winning the governorship. Concurrently, the chief justice of the Kansas Supreme Court, Bill Smith, a longtime Hall supporter and fellow Republican, considered retiring because of a lingering illness but did not want the incoming Democratic governor to fill his position. Instead, Hall, Smith, and Lieutenant Governor John McCuish executed a plan whereby Smith retired from the Kansas Supreme Court, followed quickly by Hall resigning as governor just days before Docking took office, leaving McCuish as governor to appoint Hall to Smith's vacant position on the bench. Public outrage over the so-called triple play is thought to have helped solidify the push for merit section, which was instituted the following year.

The 1960s ushered in a steady stream of states adopting merit selection for their state supreme courts, and this movement continued in the ensuing decades. Several scholars have undertaken efforts to explain this wave of adoptions. In a detailed historical treatment, Shugerman concludes that "merit succeeded in the states where business had grown powerful enough to support a campaign for merit selection, but also where labor and urban machines had not yet reached enough power to block those campaigns" (2012, 210). Furthermore, empirical studies of merit selection's diffusion highlight the importance of factors such as urbanizing states looking to maintain influence through reapportionment (Puro, Bergerson, and Puro 1985), state-specific transaction costs associated with constitutional reform (Dubois 1990a, 1990b), and the absence of entrenched political majorities with incentive to maintain the status quo (Hanssen 2004).

Currently, more than half of all states have experimented with merit selection systems for at least some of their state supreme court justices. In several states, governors have unilaterally implemented merit selection with voluntary plans (Lowe 1971; Vandenberg 1983). As of 2014, however, eighteen states had formal laws requiring the use of merit selection to fill any supreme court vacancy. In addition, seven states had formal laws requiring the use of merit selection to fill interim vacancies. Although nearly all the states that have adopted formal merit selection systems did so decades ago, the public policy debate remains vibrant as several states consider either adopting or abolishing merit selection.

Conclusion

This chapter starts with a simple question: What are merit selection's origins? The answer, however, is complex. America's history of experimentation with judicial selection institutions has been driven by contemporary political shocks and frustration with existing methods. By dispersing selection authority, Revolutionary-era constitutions built on English and colonial models of unilateral appointment. As frustration mounted with concerns about political intrigue surrounding judicial appointments, states began experimenting with elections—first the partisan variety, then nonpartisan. But these reforms were also met with criticism that the judicial selection process was too political. At the beginning of the nineteenth century, variations of what is now referred to as merit selection emerged in the scholarly literature. These proposals soon bubbled up to the political arena, where numerous states and localities considered adoption before Missouri enacted the first merit selection system for supreme court justices in 1940. After lying somewhat dormant for several years, additional states began adopting merit selection in the late 1950s.

This story of institutional development demonstrates the importance of experimentation and contemporary political shocks as determinants of reform. More generally, the story of merit selection's origins and institutionalization as a credible alternative to long-dominant methods demonstrates that concern with politicization of judicial selection has driven reform at every turn. Although reformers promised that merit selection would interrupt this historical trend by deemphasizing politics in the selection process and opening the judiciary to different types of judges, the consequences of reform are thus far unclear. The next three chapters offer a comparative institutional analysis of selection system performance across a variety of salient topics in the ongoing policy debate over judicial selection reform.

3 | Professional Experience across Selection Systems

A re certain judicial selection systems more or less likely to produce state supreme court justices with different types of professional experience? This was among the first questions posed by scholars exploring merit selection's consequences and differences across judicial selection systems more generally.[1] However, the early research in this area suffered from limited samples and analyzed differences across few employment categories. This chapter makes several contributions to our understanding of the relationship between judicial selection systems and professional experience. First, it grounds the inquiry in the developing theoretical literature on the value of experiential diversity among members of collegial courts. Second, it delineates a rich set of employment classifications, providing theoretical justifications for valuing experience in each area. Third, it improves our understanding of the link between selection institutions and the political connectedness of state supreme court justices—a primary point of emphasis in the merit selection debate. Although the results generally support previous findings of little difference in judges' experience across selection systems (e.g., Canon 1972; Glick and Emmert 1987), important differences do emerge, and the broader portrait offers significant implications for debates over state judicial selection.

Why Study Experience?

The existing literature on the connection between judicial selection institutions and professional experience lacks firm theoretical foundations. Nonetheless, understanding whether different selection systems sort on particular types of professional experience is important for several reasons. As an initial matter, interest is growing in the potential adverse effects of "career homogeneity" (Epstein, Knight, and Martin 2003, 938) among members of collegial courts (see also Barton 2012; Epstein et al. 2009; Vermeule 2007). The U.S. Supreme Court (e.g., O'Neil 2007) and state supreme courts (e.g., Borreca 2007) have been criticized for lacking experiential diversity. Some suggest that institutional performance improves when multimember bodies such as collegial courts comprise individuals with diverse professional experiences (see Epstein, Knight, and Martin 2003). The logic behind this position is that aggregating diverse perspectives improves collective decision making.[2] U.S. Supreme Court Justice Sonia Sotomayor once argued, for example, that "breadth of experience ensures . . . that every argument is aired [and] its importance deliberated."[3] Furthermore, experiential diversity may mitigate the influence of policy preferences on judicial decision making (O'Neil 2007, 732). This could occur, for example, if collegial court judges can draw from experience during the bargaining process to influence others.

A burgeoning literature on the relationship between professional experience and judicial decision making offers another reason to take this inquiry seriously. Evidence is mixed regarding whether judges with various professional backgrounds decide cases differently (see Epstein, Knight, and Martin 2003, 961–965). One study, for example, found that cases presided over by former prosecutors were no more likely to be settled or decided in favor of plaintiffs or defendants (Ashenfelter, Eisenberg, and Schwab 1995). However, a different study found that judges who had served as prosecutors were more likely to vote conservatively in cases involving civil rights, civil liberties, and economic issues (Tate and Handberg 1991). To the extent that professional experience helps explain judicial behavior, it is important to understand what determines whether individuals with different types of professional experience become judges.

The experience question can also inform our understanding of whether certain judicial selection institutions are more likely to favor individuals with strong political connections. This question has been an important part of the merit selection debate since its inception. Merit selection's proponents contend that it mitigates the importance of political connections for securing judgeships (see, e.g., Caufield 2011, 254; Glick 1978, 513; Stith and Root 2009, 748).[4] Critics, however, contend that political connections are no less important—and may even be more important—under merit selection (see, e.g., Jenks 1996, 71; Dimino 2004, 814; Shuman and Champagne 1997, 247).[5] Unfortunately, the debate regarding judicial selection institutions and political connections suffers from two limitations. First, participants rarely provide conceptual clarity with respect to what constitutes "political connections," making it difficult to know what sort of evidence could be invoked to falsify competing hypotheses. Second, attempts to empirically analyze even well-considered claims about political connections often engender considerable measurement problems.[6]

Examinations of the link between judicial selection institutions and political connections focus almost exclusively on legislative experience (see, e.g., Glick and Emmert 1987; Yelnosky 2010). The justification is that those with legislative experience are likely to have deep political ties. Nonetheless, using legislative experience as a proxy for political connectedness in the judicial selection context presents difficulties. First, legislative experience is just one manifestation of the broader concept of having held major political office. As described in more detail below, while legislative service may be the most common type of major political experience, state supreme court justices have held a variety of top-level political positions. Broadening the measurement strategy to include the array of major political positions is more consistent with commonly invoked conceptual understandings of the phrase "political connections." Moreover, this approach is consistent with a well-developed political economy literature that uses having held major political office as a proxy for political connectedness (see, e.g., Faccio 2006; Fisman and Wang 2015; Hillman 2005). Second, and more problematically, commentators often advocate for seating judges with political experience (e.g., Alleman and Mazzone 2010; Mikva 1982; Peretti 2007). As a result of contested normative positions regarding the value of seating judges with major political experience, substantive conclusions drawn from evidence concerning the link between selection institutions and this type of employment are necessarily ambiguous. Although substantial advances in our understanding of the link between judicial selection institutions and political connectedness likely require moving beyond the realm of professional experience, I introduce a new experience-based proxy leveraging ties to major political offices.

Types of Professional Experience

State supreme court justices seated from 1960 through 2014 held a variety of positions in their professional careers before joining their state high courts. This section builds on the existing literature discussing state supreme court justices' professional employment by developing a richer classification of experiential categories. Moreover, I offer theoretical rationales for why stakeholders might care about seating judges with experience in these categories. The first part discusses the distinction between private practice and public service experience. Next, I delineate important experiences within the public service category. This chapter focuses exclusively on nonjudicial professional experience. In Chapter 4, I analyze prior judicial experience as one of the qualifications motivating state supreme court seating decisions.[7]

The Public-Private Distinction

Legal employment is often divided into two broad categories: private practice and public service.[8] Although individuals may differ over the importance of prospective judges having been employed in each sector, agreement seems to be widespread that both potentially provide valuable experience. Indeed, the combination of private practice and public service experience is often praised in relation to judicial selection decisions. For example, Governor John Baldacci's justification for nominating Joseph Jabar to the Maine Supreme Court in 2009 emphasized that "Jabar has served the people of Maine through private practice and public service" (Calder 2009). Private practice is typically thought of as occurring inside a corporate entity, regardless of the number of practicing attorneys employed by the firm. Prevalent practice areas in the private sector include common law fields such contracts, property, and torts; wills, trusts, and estates; and commercial enterprise. Public service is typically thought to include governmental and public-interest employment. Although the public interest employment category is somewhat amorphous (Southworth 2013), it encompasses areas such as civil rights and liberties, indigent services, and environmental conservation.

U.S. Supreme Court Justice Stephen Breyer, who held a variety of public service positions before being appointed to the federal bench, notes that "the lawyer's public service tradition has a proud American history" (Breyer 2000, 404). Indeed, several prominent judges have urged lawyers to be active in public service. U.S. Supreme Court Justice (and later chief justice) Harlan Fiske Stone (1934) argued that lawyers should play a prominent role in public service because their special knowledge about the relationship between law and policy positioned them to improve social welfare. And in a notable 1905 speech, prominent attorney and later U.S. Supreme Court justice Louis Brandeis contrasted the "corporation lawyer" with the "people's lawyer," urging young attorneys to become the latter so that they might "protect . . . the interests of the people" (Brandeis 1905, 559).[9]

Several arguments have been advanced for why public service experience may be particularly important to acquire before joining the bench. Public service experience is sometimes treated as a proxy for having developed expertise in public law and possessing an in-depth knowledge of government institutions. Furthermore, since some attorneys struggle with the salary reduction that sometimes accompanies moves from private practice to the judiciary (see Wheeler 2010, 145–147), public service experience may serve as a credible signal of willingness to undertake long-term judicial service with reduced pay. Public service experience may also help mitigate another information asymmetry. By selecting judges "who have extensive experience in public life," stakeholders might be able to "effectively screen for vice" because longer periods of public service provide more opportunities for evidence of misconduct to surface (Solum 2005, 1386).

As with public service, while private practice experience is often lauded, its precise benefits for judicial service are not always clear beyond a general interest in promoting experiential diversity. U.S. Supreme Court Chief Justice John Roberts, for example, once suggested that having fewer judges with private practice experience "changes the nature of the federal judiciary" (Roberts 2007, 3). Although Roberts did not elaborate on the nature of this change, his predecessor William Rehnquist once offered a possible explanation when he warned that "a Judiciary composed only of those persons who are already in the public service . . . would too much resemble the judiciary in civil law countries, where a law graduate may choose upon graduation to enter the judiciary, and will thereafter gradually work his way up over time." Rehnquist added, "Reasonable people, not merely here but in Europe, think that many civil law judicial systems simply do not command the respect and enjoy the independence of ours" (Rehnquist 2002).

Valuing private practice experience in prospective judges has at least three additional justifications. As with justifications for valuing public service, however, they are based on heuristics. First, if public service employment is associated with taking progovernment positions, private practice might be associated with experience taking nongovernment perspectives. Second, private practice might be considered a proxy for trial experience and familiarity with client management. Third, private practice might be considered a proxy for experience with private law fields. Of course, these justifications break down in certain particulars: attorneys working for interest groups, in legal aid, or as public defenders often take nongovernment positions; public service lawyers may focus exclusively on trial work, while those in private practice may focus exclusively on appellate work; and public service lawyers may work in private law fields such as antitrust and securities regulation, while those in private practice may work exclusively in public law. Nonetheless, it may be reasonable to assume that private practice enjoys a net advantage over public service on these dimensions.

Public Service Varieties

"Public service" is a broad phrase that includes many different types of employment. This richness is illustrated by the varied positions once held by some who went on to become state supreme court justices.

Examples include city council member (Seymour Simon, Illinois), state budget director (Frank Sullivan, Indiana), U.S. solicitor general (Charles Fried, Massachusetts), assistant secretary of state for African Affairs (G. Mennen Williams, Michigan), legislative bill drafter (Charles Springer, Nevada), member of the U.S. Embassy in Paris (Asher William Sweeney, Ohio), mayor (Steven Taylor, Oklahoma), and special agent for the Federal Bureau of Investigation (Thomas Hawthorne Phillips, Texas). In the rest of this part, I highlight several employment categories under the public service umbrella that may interest scholars and stakeholders because of their potential implications for our understanding of judicial behavior and the debate over political connections.

Major Political Office

The American judiciary has long attracted individuals who previously held major political office. Indeed, many of the U.S. Supreme Court's best-known justices held major political positions, including Hugo Black (U.S. senator), John Marshall (secretary of state and congressperson), Sandra Day O'Connor (state legislator), Harlan Fiske Stone (U.S. attorney general), and Earl Warren (governor).[10] This is not to say that major political office holders who became U.S. Supreme Court justices necessarily went on to have remarkable judicial careers. Examples of lesser known or appreciated justices who held major political positions include Lucius Lamar (congressperson and U.S. senator), Frank Murphy (governor and U.S. attorney general), and William Woods (state legislator).

Variation in judicial performance among those who have held major political office reflects a broader debate over the efficacy of politicians becoming judges. On one side, it has been said that "political experience and skill are invaluable throughout the [judicial] decision-making process—picking the right battles, asking the right questions, crafting effective answers, knowing how to build workable coalitions inside and outside the Court, and sensing when to adjust or retreat as conditions require" (Peretti 2007, 120). According to this view, political experience can serve judges well—particularly those serving on a collegial court, such as a state supreme court, where interpersonal dynamics can profoundly shape the development of law.[11] Furthermore, scholars have championed seating judges with major political experience because of their presumed record of appealing to large constituencies and acute knowledge of government's inner workings, both of which may add important perspective to a collegial decision-making environment (Mikva 1982; Alleman and Mazzone 2010).

But not everyone is sanguine about drawing judges from the pool of candidates having held major political office. Evidence suggests that stakeholders do not consider political experience to be an important judicial qualification. Indeed, citizens (Petrie 1974, 3854), judges (Sheldon 1968), and merit selection commissioners (Caufield 2012, 3) have all suggested that political experience matters little if at all in determining whether someone is qualified to be a judge. In one survey, for example, state trial court judges ranked political experience the least important qualification "by a very wide margin" (M. Rosenberg 1966, 1068). Furthermore, voters asked about their view of judicial qualifications revealed that "prior political experience was one of the least important factors and . . . most voters who did say it was important preferred candidates to not have prior political experience" (Simmons 2012, 37). Other opposition arguments include concern that putting high-profile politicians on the bench may negatively influence perceptions of institutional legitimacy and hinder judicial performance (Denning 2012).[12]

Having held major political office is also an issue in the debate over judicial selection institutions because it signals the depth of one's political connections (see, e.g., Emmert and Glick 1988; Slotnick 1984; Yelnosky 2010).[13] As noted previously, competing claims have been made about the importance of political connections for securing judgeships through merit selection. Most of the empirical studies on the relationship between judicial selection institutions and political connections focus exclusively on legislative experience (Canon 1972; Glick and Emmert 1987; Jacob 1964). In general, these studies reveal two things. First, legislative appointment states are more likely to produce state supreme court justices with legislative experience. Second, aside from this result, there is little difference in the production of state supreme court justices with prior legislative experience across selection institutions.

From 1960 through 2014, justices with legislative experience filled about 15 percent of state supreme court openings. Most of these previously served in their state legislatures. Although the two states that currently use legislative appointment (South Carolina and Virginia) continue to draw a considerable number of their supreme court justices from the pool of individuals with legislative experience, former legislators also make the transition under other systems. Recently, for example, former state legislators joined their state high courts through merit selection (Andrew McDonald, Connecticut) and gubernatorial appointment (Correale Stevens, Pennsylvania). In addition to state legislative experience, some state supreme court justices served in Congress. For example, Charles Canady, who had also served in the Florida legislature, served four terms in the U.S. House before abiding by a self-imposed term limit. After leaving Congress, Canady became Florida governor Jeb Bush's general counsel and shortly thereafter was appointed to an intermediate appellate court where he served until being appointed to the Florida Supreme Court through merit selection.

Although less well recognized, no doubt as a result of being less common, state supreme court justices also arrive having held prominent executive branch positions. William Howard Taft is the best-known example of someone going from a prominent executive branch position to a high court position, having served one term as president of the United States before President Warren Harding appointed him to the position he had long coveted—chief justice of the U.S. Supreme Court. At the state level, about 1 percent of openings were filled by former governors, 3 percent by former attorneys general, and 2 percent by individuals who had held other top-level executive positions such as lieutenant governor or secretary of state. John King, who had also served as a state legislator, was the most recent former governor to make the transition when he joined the New Hampshire Supreme Court in 1979. In 2010, William Mims, who had also served in both houses of the state legislature, became the most recent attorney general to make the transition when he joined the Virginia Supreme Court. And Maureen O'Connor was elected to the Ohio Supreme Court in 2002 after serving as lieutenant governor.

The perception that justices with major-office experience secured their state supreme court judgeships by leveraging political connections regularly generates considerable controversy, particularly in states that use merit selection or elite appointment. The Kansas "triple play" discussed in Chapter 2 is one example. James Brickley's 1982 appointment to the Michigan Supreme Court by Republican governor William Milliken provides another example of controversy fueled by the perception that political connections dictated a judicial selection decision (Dempsey 2006, 220–233). Brickley had been Milliken's lieutenant governor on two separate occasions, and Milliken had backed his good friend's effort to succeed him as governor in 1982. However, Brickley was defeated in the primary, and Republican Jim Blanchard won the November election. Although Blanchard was expecting to fill a state supreme court position that became vacant in December, Milliken swore Brickley into the position two days before leaving the governor's office.[14]

Major-Office Ties

While the literature on judicial selection institutions and experience primarily employs legislative experience as a proxy for political connectedness, having ties to major political office through subordinate employment positions is an alternative measure. Unlike the argument for selecting judges with major political experience, the argument for why having ties to major political office should improve judicial decision making is more tenuous. Examples of these subordinate positions include governor's counsel, legislative aide, and assistant attorney general. Although the path from political subordinate to state supreme court justice may not be direct, the connections developed while serving important officeholders can prove pivotal. This is evidenced by Governor Warren Rudman's appointment of David Souter to the New Hampshire Supreme Court. In 1982, U.S. senator and former New Hampshire attorney general Warren Rudman helped John Sununu win New Hampshire's gubernatorial race (Yarbrough 2005, 62). On election night, Sununu reportedly told Rudman, "Anything you want in this state, you've got." Rudman responded by asking Sununu to appoint David Souter, Rudman's former deputy in the attorney general's office, to the New Hampshire Supreme Court, to which

Sununu reportedly replied, "It's done" (62). Subsequently, Sununu became President George H. W. Bush's chief of staff, and both he and Rudman were instrumental in Bush nominating Souter to the U.S. Court of Appeals for the First Circuit and later to the U.S. Supreme Court (94–146).

Sometimes the political connection is more direct and controversial. Several governors, for example, have faced criticism for appointing their former counsels to supreme court positions (see, e.g., Baye 2014; Ramsey 2012). In 2014, Kansas governor Sam Brownback unilaterally appointed his chief counsel, Caleb Stegall, to a position on the Kansas Court of Appeals in a move one political opponent called "the worst kind of political cronyism" (Lowry 2014a).[15] When a vacancy arose on the Kansas Supreme Court about six months later, Stegall applied for the position, and his name was forwarded by the nominating commission to the governor, along with the names of two state judges with nearly fifty years of combined judicial experience. At that point, political opponents claimed that Stegall's appointment was a "foregone conclusion" (Lowry 2014a). When Brownback formally selected Stegall about two weeks later, supporters praised his "unique skill set" as a former executive branch employee, while critics called it the "last gasp of a failed governor who knows his time in office is coming to an end," adding that the governor "put his own political agenda before the best interests of Kansans" by selecting "his political ally with less than nine months of judicial experience" over "a judge with more than 20 years on the bench" (Lowry 2014b).

Prosecutors

State supreme court justices often have prosecutorial experience (e.g., Bonneau 2001; Canon 1972; Glick and Emmert 1987). Prosecutors play a central role in the criminal justice system, enjoying "formidable power and vast discretion" (A. Davis 2007, 4). A prosecutor's responsibilities may include managing office resources, deciding which crimes will be office priorities, working with law enforcement, making charging decisions, engaging in plea negotiations, and overseeing trials. That there are a variety of prosecutorial positions is well illustrated by examining the professional experiences compiled by state supreme court justices. Commonly held positions at the state level include assistant district attorney and district attorney, and commonly held positions at the federal level include U.S. attorney and assistant U.S. attorney.[16]

Several justifications have been offered for valuing prosecutorial experience in a prospective judge. When Sonia Sotomayor was nominated to the U.S. Supreme Court, for example, Senator Amy Klobuchar declared, "Sotomayor's experience as a prosecutor tells me she . . . is someone who deeply appreciates the power and impact that laws have and that the criminal justice system has on real people's lives" ("Sotomayor Nomination" 2009, S6978). Depth of courtroom experience is another commonly noted justification for valuing prosecutorial service. Upon nominating a prosecutor to a state judgeship, for example, Hawaii governor Linda Lingle explained that the individual's "extensive experience as a prosecutor . . . [had imparted] a thorough understanding of courtroom procedure and the judicial process" ("Governor Lingle" 2009).

Governor Lingle offered another justification for valuing prosecutorial experience in prospective judges on a different occasion. Explaining her proclivity to appoint judges with prosecutorial experience, Lingle emphasized her preference "to bring in [judges] who believe that victims' rights are more important than criminals' rights" (Borreca 2007). Texas Court of Criminal Appeals judge and former prosecutor Sharon Keller once put it more bluntly when she referred to herself as "pro-prosecutor," adding that this "means . . . seeing legal issues from the perspective of the state instead of the perspective of the defense" (Michael Hall 2009).[17] Others, however, have observed that prosecutorial experience may cut the other way, enhancing concern for defendant rights in an effort to ensure due process (Wingfield 2009). Most notably, U.S. Supreme Court chief justice Earl Warren's prosecutorial experience is regularly referred to when explaining his interest in affording defendants enhanced constitutional protections (see Schwartz 1997).[18]

Federal Government

Most state supreme court justices with governmental experience served exclusively in state or local capacities. Although this emphasis is understandable, experience serving in the federal government may offer benefits as well. For example, this experience may be thought to add an important perspective to the bench given that state supreme court justices regularly interpret and apply federal law. Furthermore, some have suggested that seating justices with federal experience may enhance a state supreme court's national prestige (see, e.g., Dolan 2014). As previously noted, state supreme court justices had been members of Congress, U.S. attorneys, or assistant U.S. attorneys. Other state supreme court justices with federal government experience had a colorful array of titles, including special assistant to the deputy secretary of the U.S. Department of Education (Goodwin Liu, California), senior advisor to the under secretary of Enforcement at the U.S. Department of the Treasury (Mariano-Florentino Cuellar, California), enforcement attorney at the Environmental Protection Agency (Gregory Hobbs, Colorado), legislative assistant to a U.S. senator (David Prosser, Wisconsin), and assistant counsel to the U.S. Senate Public Works Committee (Margaret Workman, West Virginia).

Academic Experience

The literature on professional experience and judicial decision making places comparatively little emphasis on judges having been full-time faculty members. However, the subject's leading study suggests that "academic experience could create an 'individualistic' judge, one who is more active and independent than her colleagues" (George 2001, 15). Many U.S. Supreme Court justices previously served as full-time professors. For example, Justices Breyer, Ruth Bader Ginsburg, and Antonin Scalia were all prominent law professors. Although no justice has joined the U.S. Supreme Court directly from a full-time academic position since President Roosevelt nominated Felix Frankfurter to the bench in 1939, it occasionally occurs in the states.[19] David Stras was a law professor at the University of Minnesota before joining the Minnesota Supreme Court in 2010, Thomas Lee (son of former U.S. solicitor general Rex Lee and brother of U.S. senator Mike Lee) was a law professor at Brigham Young University before joining the Utah Supreme Court in 2010, and Goodwin Liu was a law professor at University of California at Berkeley before joining the California Supreme Court in 2011.[20] Each of these justices was appointed to the bench.[21]

Legal Services

Legal services for the poor and underrepresented is a pressing issue in law and society (e.g., Abel 1985; Lawrence 1990; Ogletree 1993). Individuals with experience working in areas involving legal services may bring special insight to the bench regarding the challenges faced by the indigent and underrepresented with respect to information acquisition, securing representation, court access, and case management. Public defender is one example of a position that falls under this heading. These attorneys represent indigent defendants in the criminal justice system. Legal aid is another category that falls under the legal services umbrella. The legal aid category comprises a variety of positions dedicated to assisting indigent and underrepresented clients. For example, Justice Jenny Rivera, who was appointed to New York's highest court in 2013, previously served as an attorney for the Legal Aid Society's Homeless Family Rights Project and as counsel to the Puerto Rican Legal Defense and Education Fund.

Empirical Analysis

To examine whether different judicial selection systems produce state supreme court justices with different types of professional experience, I compiled a database of state supreme court justices seated from 1960 through 2014 as described in Appendix A. There were 1,525 individuals seated on state supreme courts during the sample period and 1,543 seating events (18 individuals were seated on two separate occasions). After compiling this database, I searched biographical records for information about the professional positions these individuals held before becoming state supreme court justices. I obtained extensive information about professional experience for all but 20 justices (98.7 percent of the seatings) and partial information for two others.[22] Although existing research on judicial background experience often accounts only for the position held immediately before becoming a judge, these data include information on all prior professional positions. As a result, justices can be included in more than one category with the exception of the public-private distinction, according to which all but one justice (who did not have any pre-judicial experience) fell into one of three categories: public service only, private practice only, or public service and private practice experience.[23]

Dependent Variables

The dependent variables correspond to the categories of professional experience developed previously: only public service, only private practice, public service and private practice, major political office, major-office ties, prosecutor, federal government, academic, and legal services. Figure 3.1 plots the percentage of state supreme court seatings from 1960 through 2014 with experience in each category. Academia is the least common employment category, with about 4 percent of justices having full-time experience in this area.[24] About 54 percent had experience in the public and private sectors, making it the only employment category to include a majority of the justices.[25] In comparison, 14 percent of justices served only in the public sector, while 33 percent served only in the private sector. That 18 percent of justices

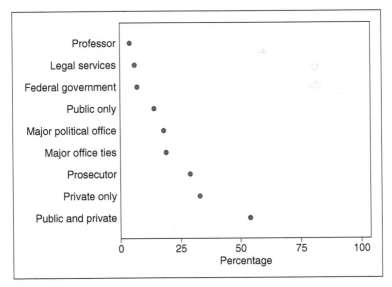

Figure 3.1 Summary statistics: experience

held major political office is also notable. Overall, the lack of strong clustering within one category suggests that there is no single professional path leading to service on state supreme courts.

Independent Variables

The key explanatory variables capture judicial selection institutions. As discussed in Chapter 1, judicial selection mechanisms can vary within a single state because of differing institutional arrangements for regular and interim seatings. Thus, these variables are coded at the justice level rather than the state level. The appointment variable is scored one for justices who were appointed to their seats (without the aid of a commission) and zero otherwise.[26] The election variable is scored one for justices who were seated through partisan or nonpartisan election and zero otherwise. The excluded baseline captures justices who were seated through merit selection. Figure 3.2 displays the percentage of seatings within each category of the public-private distinction by selection system. Figure 3.3 displays the percentage of seatings within different public service occupations by selection system.

Several control variables are included to account for the possibility that certain features of a state's political and institutional environment are correlated both with the primary explanatory variables and the dependent variables. Individuals with certain types of professional experience may perceive state supreme court positions to be more or less valuable.[27] As a result, I account for institutional rules that may affect the perceived value of securing a state supreme court position (cf. Bratton and Spill 2002).[28] First, I include Peverill Squire's (2008) state supreme court professionalism index, which incorporates information regarding salary, the number of available law clerks, and discretionary docket control. Second, I include a variable counting the number of supreme court seats. Third, I include a variable counting the number of years in a justice's term.[29] Last, I include a variable scored one if a mandatory retirement rule was in place and zero otherwise.

To capture the size of the eligibility pool, which may influence the likelihood of drawing supreme court justices with certain types of experience, I include a variable scoring the natural log of the number of attorneys in a state.[30] Given that selectors with varying ideological

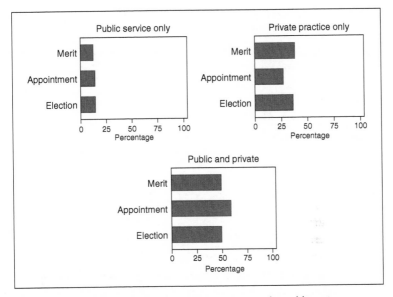

Figure 3.2 Summary statistics by selection system: the public-private distinction

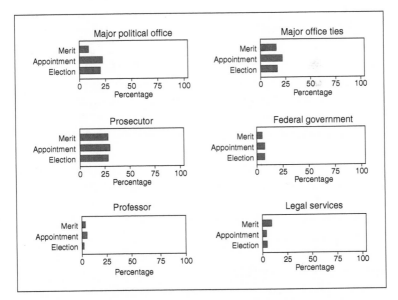

Figure 3.3 Summary statistics by selection system: public service varieties

preferences may prefer justices with certain types of professional experience (cf. Holmes 2012), I include a measure of state ideology that ranges from most conservative to most liberal (Berry et al. 1998).[31] I also include controls to account for regional and temporal variation in seating state supreme court justices with different professional backgrounds (Glick and Emmert 1987). To account for regional variation, I include region fixed effects.[32] To account for temporal variation, I include a cubic polynomial approximation (Carter and Signorino 2010).[33]

Analysis and Results

Given that each dependent variable is binary, I fit the models with logistic regression. Standard errors are clustered by state to account for nonindependence within states. For interested readers, Tables B1 and B2 in Appendix B present full results from a series of logistic regressions explaining the probability of seating a state supreme court justice with each type of professional experience. Although the estimated coefficients and standard errors presented in these tables provide information about statistical significance, they do not convey readily interpretable information about substantive impact. To provide easy-to-interpret information about substantive differences across selection systems, Table 3.1 presents changes in the predicted probability associated with seating a justice with experience in a particular category moving from the first selection institution to the second.[34] Table 3.1 also includes 95 percent confidence intervals around the predicted change in probability, indicating whether the difference is statistically distinguishable from zero at that threshold.

Overall, there are more similarities than differences across selection systems in terms of the types of professional experience compiled by individuals before becoming state supreme court justices. Of the twenty-seven pairwise comparisons across selection institutions and experience categories, ten yield differences that are statistically distinguishable from zero. Furthermore, there were no differences across selection institutions in the public service and legal services categories.

Notwithstanding the similarities across selection systems, several differences are worth noting. As an initial matter, elite appointment is

TABLE 3.1 CHANGE IN QUANTITIES OF INTEREST: EXPERIENCE

	Merit vs. appointment	Merit vs. election	Appointment vs. election
Public service only	1% (–4%, 5%)	2% (–4%, 7%)	1% (–3%, 5%)
Private practice only	–10%* (–16%, –3%)	–2% (–10%, 6%)	8%* (2%, 14%)
Public and private	9%* (3%, 16%)	≈0% (–7%, 8%)	–9%* (–15%, –3%)
Major political office	11%* (5%, 18%)	15%* (8%, 21%)	3% (–4%, 11%)
Major office ties	9%* (4%, 15%)	5% (–1%, 12%)	–4% (–10%, 2%)
Prosecutor	2%* (1%, 3%)	1% (–1%, 2%)	–1% (–2%, 1%)
Federal government	3%* (1%, 7%)	2% (–2%, 6%)	–1% (–4%, 2%)
Professor	1% (–1%, 3%)	–1% (–3%, 1%)	–2%* (–4%, –1%)
Legal services	≈0% (–1%, 1%)	≈0% (–1%, 1%)	≈0% (–1%, 1%)

Note: Numbers outside parentheses are changes in predicted probabilities moving from the first selection system to the second. Parentheses contain 95 percent confidence intervals. Results from the full models that generated these results are presented in Tables B1 and B2 in Appendix B.
*$p < 0.05$ (two-tailed).

less likely than merit selection and election to produce state supreme court justices who have private practice but not public service experience. The predicted probability of seating a justice with only private practice experience decreases from 36 percent (95 percent confidence interval of 29 percent, 42 percent) under merit selection to 26 percent (22 percent, 29 percent) under appointment, a change of –10 percent (–16 percent, –3 percent). Furthermore, the predicted probability of seating a justice with only private practice experience increases from 26 percent (22 percent, 29 percent) under appointment to 34 percent (27 percent, 40 percent) under election, a change of 8 percent (2 percent, 14 percent). These results suggest that having public service experience is particularly important for state supreme court vacancies filled by elite appointment. However, having only public service experience is not associated with a significant change in the probability of being seated across any pairwise comparison of selection systems.

Having both public service and private practice experience is associated with an increase in the predicted probability of becoming a state supreme court justice in appointment states. Substantively, the predicted probability of seating a justice with public service and private practice experience increases from 52 percent (46 percent, 58 percent) under merit selection to 61 percent (57 percent, 66 percent) under appointment, a change of 9 percent (3 percent, 16 percent). Furthermore, the predicted probability of seating a justice with public service and private practice experience decreases from 61 percent (57 percent, 66 percent) under appointment to 52 percent (46 percent, 58 percent) under election, a change of –9 percent (–15 percent, –3 percent). To the extent that an individual's experiential diversity is valued, these results portend an important advantage for elite appointment. However, the likely trade-off is that seated justices have less experience on average in private practice.

The results for major political office suggest that individuals with this experience are less likely to be seated in merit selection states. Substantively, the predicted probability of someone with major-office experience being seated increases from 9 percent (5 percent, 12 percent) under merit selection to 20 percent (14 percent, 26 percent) under appointment, a change of 11 percent (5 percent, 18 percent). To examine whether this result was driven by states that use legislative appointment, I fit another model disaggregating the appointment category. The results from this alternative specification suggest that individuals with major-office experience are more likely to be seated under legislative and nonlegislative appointment relative to merit selection, but the difference between legislative and nonlegislative appointment is not statistically distinguishable from zero. Those with major-office experience are also more likely to be seated under election than under merit selection. Substantively, the predicted probability of seating someone with major-office experience increases from 9 percent (5 percent, 12 percent) under merit selection to 24 percent (17 percent, 30 percent) under election, a change of 15 percent (8 percent, 21 percent). As discussed previously, the normative implications of these results depend on the value imputed to seating judges with major political experience. While some may argue that these results suggest that merit selection is less likely to favor those with political connections, others may argue that having more justices with this type of experience would be a net positive for the judiciary.

Previously, I suggested that we might gain additional leverage over the political connections question by looking at individuals with major-office ties since this pool of candidates is likely to have strong connections while experience in these positions is not considered to be as inherently valuable as having held major political office. The predicted probability of seating a justice with major-office ties increases from 13 percent (8 percent, 18 percent) under merit selection to 22 percent (18 percent, 27 percent) under appointment, a change of 9 percent (4 percent, 15 percent).[35] However, the differences when comparing merit selection to election and appointment to election are not statistically distinguishable from zero.

Three other differences between selection systems are worth noting, but in each case the difference is substantively small. First, the predicted probability of seating someone with prosecutorial experience increases from 1 percent (<1 percent, >1 percent) under merit selection to 3 percent (1 percent, 4 percent) under appointment, a change of 2 percent (1 percent, 3 percent). Second, the predicted probability of seating someone with experience working for the federal government increases from 4 percent (2 percent, 6 percent) under merit selection to 7 percent (5 percent, 10 percent) under appointment, a change of 3 percent (1 percent, 7 percent).[36] Third, the predicted probability of seating someone with academic experience decreases from 4 percent (2 percent, 6 percent) under appointment to 2 percent (1 percent, 3 percent) under election, a change of –2 percent (–4 percent, –1 percent).[37]

None of the control variables are consistently associated with seating state supreme court justices who have certain types of professional experience. However, two control variables are associated with more than one outcome of interest. An increase in state liberalism from one standard deviation below its mean to one standard deviation above is associated with an increase in the predicted probability of seating a state supreme court justice with only public service experience from 8 percent (5 percent, 12 percent) to 16 percent (12 percent,

20 percent), a change of 8 percent (3 percent, 12 percent). Although the estimated coefficient for the state liberalism variable is also statistically significant in the legal services model, a change from one standard deviation below the mean state liberalism score to one standard deviation above yields a difference that is not statistically distinguishable from zero. An increase in court professionalism from one standard deviation below its mean to one standard deviation above is associated with a decrease in the predicted probability of seating an individual with ties to major political office from 26 percent (21 percent, 32 percent) to 19 percent (14 percent, 24 percent), a change of -7 percent (-13 percent, -1 percent). Furthermore, the same increase in court professionalism is associated with a decrease in the probability of seating someone with federal government experience from 9 percent (5 percent, 12 percent) to 23 percent (17 percent, 30 percent), a change of 14 percent (8 percent, 21 percent).

In the private practice model, an increase in the natural log of lawyers in a state from one standard deviation below the mean to one standard deviation above is associated with an increase in the probability of seating someone with only private practice experience from 14 percent (8 percent, 21 percent) to 42 percent (30 percent, 54 percent), a change of 28 percent (11 percent, 45 percent). The existence of a mandatory retirement provision is associated with an increase in the probability of seating someone with major political experience from 13 percent (8 percent, 19 percent) to 20 percent (14 percent, 26 percent), a change of 7 percent (1 percent, 13 percent). Although the estimated coefficient for the court size variable is statistically significant in the federal government experience model, a change from its minimum (three seats) to maximum (nine seats) yields a difference that is not statistically distinguishable from zero.

Conclusion

This chapter makes contributions to our understanding of the link between judicial selection institutions and the professional experience amassed by state supreme court justices. Overall, there are more similarities than differences across selection systems in terms of the types of work experience compiled by state supreme court justices.

Moreover, no selection system is more or less likely than any other to systematically favor justices across experience categories. This suggests that justices with a range of experiences are seated under each system. Given that preferences differ over what types of experience should be valued most highly, any normative implications derived from the results presented here are likely to be contested. For example, those who think prior public service employment should be a prerequisite for becoming a judge might favor appointment over merit selection and election. Those who think there is real value in seating justices who have held major political office, meanwhile, might favor election or appointment over merit selection. Although debates concerning the normative value of different pre-judicial career paths are beyond the scope of this project, the results presented here are informative for those interested in these discussions and in experiential diversity more broadly.

The results also offer interesting insights into the debate over the extent to which different selection systems favor individuals with strong political connections. As discussed previously, the existing literature on this question has focused almost exclusively on having prior legislative experience. Broadening the inquiry here to include major political offices, the results suggest that a smaller percentage of justices seated under merit selection have this experience than justices seated through appointment or election—a finding that holds even after accounting for legislative selection. As a proxy for the ongoing debate over judicial selection and political connections, this evidence may suggest that merit selection is performing well. However, as noted previously, many argue that having held major political office is an important and underrepresented qualification for judicial office. From this perspective, evidence that a smaller percentage of justices seated under merit selection have held major political office might be considered a point against merit selection in terms of fostering experiential diversity.

To advance the debate over political connections, I also examine whether there are differences across selection systems in terms of individuals with employment ties to major political offices. Although many argue that important benefits are associated with favoring those who have held major political office for judicial vacancies, those benefits are more tenuous when it comes to holding subordinate positions. Moreover, there is a clear theoretical link between occupying these positions and possessing important political connections. The results suggest that a higher percentage of justices seated under appointment have employment ties to major political offices than justices seated through merit selection or election. Ultimately, as with the results on having held major political office, the decision about how to interpret this information depends in part on the extent to which these are considered reasonable proxies for political connectedness. Interpretation also depends on the extent to which one thinks experience in these positions to be otherwise valuable.

Two issues related to merit selection and the political connectedness of state supreme court justices require additional attention. First, some effort should be made to develop clear ex ante conceptualizations of the phrase "political connections" that distinguish between theoretically relevant and irrelevant background characteristics and experience. Of course, reasonable people will differ over their understanding of what constitutes political connections in this context, but shifting the debate to this front would improve the status quo of relying on an otherwise analytically bereft phrase to drive such an important policy discussion. Second, when the phrase "political connections" rests on firmer conceptual footing, scholars can more fruitfully turn to the considerable measurement problem that plagues empirical analysis in this area.

One potentially promising avenue for future research is to look beyond previous employment for indicators of political connections. In the political economy literature, for example, scholars have looked to political contributions (e.g., Claessens, Feijen, and Laeven 2008; Ferguson and Voth 2008; Ovtchinnikov and Pantaleoni 2012) and family ties (e.g., Faccio, Masulis, and McConnell 2006) as ways to empirically capture political connections beyond the employment context.[38] Scholars have already demonstrated the promise of employing data on political donations made by state supreme court justices (Bonica and Woodruff 2015).[39] Moreover, numerous state supreme court justices have politically relevant family ties.[40] These approaches may be improvements over experience-based proxies insofar as they attempt to capture connections independent from characteristics that reasonable observers might consider important (and a plausible case can be made for virtually any previous professional employment) when determining whether to seat someone on a state supreme court.[41]

As the literature on judicial background experience progresses, it will be important to obtain more nuanced data over longer periods. The existing literature is currently lacking in at least two respects. First, little information is available about the length of time judges spend in various positions, and this lack of data is especially glaring as one moves further back in time. Currently, for example, there is little opportunity to distinguish someone who spent, say, six months as a prosecutor from someone who spent twenty years in the same position. Second, biographical materials rarely mention varieties of private practice experience, often simply noting instead that the person engaged in "private practice."[42] And here too the scarcity of information is particularly problematic as one moves further back in time. Although the phrase "private practice" is a useful organizational heuristic, it encompasses many different types of employment. These alternative environments may provide important but different types of experiences. Moreover, attorneys in private practice cover almost the entire range of legal fields. As with public service, experience with different areas of private practice may generate different expectations about judicial performance and stakeholder evaluations of relevant expertise.

4 | Seating Qualified Justices

oes merit selection produce better-qualified judges? This has been the core question underlying the policy debate over merit selection since its inception. Indeed, using a commission to narrow a field of judicial candidates before elite nomination was called merit selection to convey the notion that this institutional arrangement would generate a more qualified judiciary. This allows proponents to suggest that merit selection produces better-qualified judges by definition. As the American Judicature Society puts it, the system "is called 'merit selection' because the judicial nomination commission chooses applicants on the basis of their qualifications, not on the basis of political or social connections" (American Judicature Society, n.d.). On the other hand, one critic summarized the opposing position by calling merit selection a "propagandistic misnomer" because of the lack of evidence that it produces better-qualified judges (Dimino 2004, 803).

Ultimately, whether merit selection produces better-qualified judges is an empirical question. Previous efforts to answer it suffered from data or methodological limitations that severely limit our ability to draw firm inferences about the relationship between a state's choice of judicial selection institution and judicial qualifications. In this chapter, I bring new data to bear on this important question. Before addressing it, however, I situate the contemporary discussion over merit selection in historical context, demonstrating that America's centuries-old debate over judicial selection has focused predominantly on qualifications at every turn. In light of this debate's centrality to the politics of institutional design and the quality of the judiciary, it is important to provide convincing empirical foundations for stakeholders to draw from in future debates. Overall, the results presented in this chapter reveal that no method of selecting judges consistently outperforms the others.

The Historical Debate over Judicial Qualifications

The American focus on judicial qualifications is long standing. The colonial practice of Crown representatives unilaterally appointing judges on the basis of political connections and patronage led to deep frustration with courts during this era (Surrency 1967). One contemporary colonial account complained of Crown-appointed judges who "know little law and give no direction to the jury nor sum up the evidences to them" while conducting "proceedings [that] are many times very arbitrary and contrary to the laws of the place" (Headlam 1908, 543). Another contemporary account lamented "a pretended Court of Justice appointed by [the Governor]" with an "illiterate Chief Judge" and assistants who were largely "unqualified by law" (222). Law was a nascent profession in colonial America, and few people had formal legal training (Provine 1986). But the increase in economic complexity and growth during this time and into the early eighteenth century fostered the legal field's development as a profession. Furthermore, as economic interconnectedness brought more people to the courts, there was an increased emphasis on the technical aspects of legal rules and a commitment to following procedure rather than resting judgments on sometimes arbitrary conceptions of justice (K. Hall 1989).

During the Revolutionary era, states responded to frustrations over the inadequacies of colonial judicial selection by drafting constitutions that divided appointment power among multiple authorities. The next focused discussion concerning the relationship between judicial selection institutions and judicial qualifications occurred during the

Constitutional Convention. James Wilson, a prominent lawyer and later U.S. Supreme Court justice, complained that "intrigue, partiality, and concealment were the necessary consequences" of having legislatures appoint judges.[1] This prompted Benjamin Franklin to call for delegates to suggest judicial selection methods other than appointment by the legislative or executive branches, referring to the question as "a point of great moment" and playfully relaying the Scottish practice by "which the nomination proceeded from the Lawyers, who always selected the ablest of the profession in order to get rid of him, and share his practice among themselves."[2] James Madison concluded this brief discussion by echoing Wilson's concerns about legislative appointment, adding that "many of [those selected this way] were not judges of the requisite qualifications" and that "the Legislative talents which were very different from those of a Judge, commonly recommended men to the favor of Legislative Assemblies."[3] Aside from this cursory exchange, delegates did not dwell on the subject of judicial qualifications. Indeed, the U.S. Constitution does not even specify minimum qualifications such as age for judges as it does for the president and members of Congress (Vile and Perez-Reilly 1991). But this does not mean that delegates were not interested in the question of judicial qualifications. Rather, they might have simply "assum[ed] viva voce and sub silentio that merit, as opposed to favoritism, should and, indeed, would govern quite naturally" (Abraham 2008, 20).

During the ratification debates, Alexander Hamilton wrote at length about judicial qualifications as Publius in "Federalist No. 76." Specifically, Hamilton defended the U.S. Constitution's delegation of judicial nomination authority to a single person (the president) rather than a group (such as Congress):

> The sole and undivided responsibility of one man will naturally beget a livelier sense of duty and a more exact regard to reputation. He will, on this account, feel himself under stronger obligations, and more interested to investigate with care the qualities requisite to the stations to be filled, and to prefer with impartiality the persons who may have the fairest pretensions to them. He will have fewer personal attachments to gratify, than a body of men who may each be supposed to have an equal

number; and will be so much the less liable to be misled by the sentiments of friendship and of affection. A single well-directed man, by a single understanding, cannot be distracted and warped by that diversity of views, feelings, and interests, which frequently distract and warp the resolutions of a collective body. There is nothing so apt to agitate the passions of mankind as personal considerations whether they relate to ourselves or to others, who are to be the objects of our choice or preference. Hence, in every exercise of the power of appointing to offices, by an assembly of men, we must expect to see a full display of all the private and party likings and dislikes, partialities and antipathies, attachments and animosities, which are felt by those who compose the assembly. The choice which may at any time happen to be made under such circumstances, will of course be the result either of a victory gained by one party over the other, or of a compromise between the parties. In either case, the intrinsic merit of the candidate will be too often out of sight. (Hamilton 1788)

While emphasizing the president's comparative advantage over Congress in nominating meritorious public officials, however, Hamilton also recognized the value of checking unilateral authority. Although Hamilton suggested that "it is . . . not very probable that [the president's] nomination would often be overruled," he argued that "the necessity of [the Senate's] concurrence would have a powerful, though, in general, a silent operation" and "would be an excellent check upon a spirit of favoritism in the President, and would tend greatly to prevent the appointment of unfit characters from State prejudice, from family connection, from personal attachment, or from a view to popularity."

Although the primary federal judicial selection institutions have remained stable since the Constitution's ratification, efforts have been made to infuse merit into the process. The Eisenhower administration, for example, pushed for the American Bar Association (ABA) to play a more systematic role in evaluating federal judicial nominees, an evaluation in part based on merit in an effort to counteract political pressures to nominate underqualified candidates with political connections (Little 2001). The ABA's formal evaluation criteria include integrity, professional competence, and judicial temperament.[4] Shortly after taking office, President Jimmy Carter issued an executive order creating circuit-based nominating commissions charged with identifying qualified candidates to fill circuit court openings.[5] Subsequently, President Carter issued a second executive order encouraging senators to create commissions for evaluating potential district court nominees.[6] Critics have contended that President Carter was more interested in enhancing gender and racial diversity on the federal courts than in finding the most qualified candidates (see Slotnick 1983). While President Carter certainly succeeded in diversifying the federal judiciary (Goldman 1978), the extent to which his nominations were otherwise more meritorious remains an open question (S. Davis 1986). President Ronald Reagan revoked Carter's executive orders establishing and encouraging the use of nominating commissions, but some district court commissions are still in use.[7]

Notwithstanding modest experimentation with judicial selection institutions at the federal level, the states have been leaders at innovating institutional arrangements concerning judicial selection for more than a century. When states began seriously considering judicial elections midway through the nineteenth century, debate centered on qualifications. Proponents of judicial elections argued in part that the people were knowledgeable and best situated to select qualified judges because their interests were ultimately at stake (e.g., K. Hall 1983; N. Nelson 1993; Shugerman 2012). As one delegate to the Massachusetts Constitutional Convention of 1853 argued, "All will agree that we, the people, have the right to elect our judiciary as we elect the other departments of government," and the people "always will have sufficient intelligence and discrimination to make a proper selection" with respect to "ascertaining the qualifications of their judiciary" (*Official Report* 1853, 235).[8] Another delegate to the same convention emphasized the importance of recognizing the connection between judges and the people, suggesting that "judges are placed in a position in the discharge of their duties, which makes them stand out more conspicuous than any other class, and their characters are better understood, are more open to discussion and scrutiny, and the people can judge better of their ability, integrity, and personal honor, than almost any other class of men" (241).

Proponents of judicial elections also emphasized the political nature of appointments. One delegate to the Massachusetts Convention spoke at length on this issue:

> [Judicial] appointments are often confined to cliques and circles of a few politicians, who dictate the appointments, and those who do not belong to them, however well qualified they may be, can never hope to rise to the bench. They are frequently made as rewards for party services. And the man who stands upon his own personal merits and reputation, independent of cliques and parties, has no chance. He must give a *quid pro quo* in the nature of party services. But make the judges elective by the people, and if a man has ability, honesty, and legal reputation, the people will find it out, and in that way they will break up this kind of cliqueism which will always be found to prevail wherever the present mode of appointment exists. (*Official Report* 1853, 237)

The sentiment that appointing authorities often let politics interfere with selecting the most qualified judges influenced other states during this period as well. In New York, which set off a wave of reform by adopting judicial elections in 1850, delegates to the Constitutional Convention of 1846 complained that the judicial appointment process had been corrupted. One delegate, for example, lamented "political appointments to the judicial office" and argued that "the ermine had been tarnished, and our judiciary system brought in reproach . . . by the appointment of a number of stupid and incapable men as judges, who were common political brawlers" (Bishop and Attree 1846, 613).

Foreshadowing some of the arguments against judicial elections that are prominent today, opponents of reform during the mid-nineteenth century voiced concern that judicial qualifications would suffer under an elective system. In New York, for example, one delegate noted his "firm conviction . . . that a choice made by the spontaneous, independent, impartial action of the electoral body of this State, would place in your judicial tribunals incumbents as well qualified as any that could be procured in any mode that has been or can be devised" (Bishop and Attree 1846, 790). Nonetheless, he went on to make the case against judicial elections on the assumption that parties would control the process and put politics ahead of merit: "We all know that nominations to these offices will be made, as others are, by party caucuses and conventions—we know that these assemblages, and the nominations they make, are very often the result of intrigue, of management, of personal and local arrangements and of the contracts and bargains of mere politicians" (790).

Others thought law's complexity rendered laypersons incapable of selecting the most qualified individuals for judgeships. One delegate to the Illinois Constitutional Convention of 1847, for example, argued that "he had as high an opinion of the general intelligence of the people as any man, but he would not flatter the people by attributing to them qualifications which they did not as a body possess, nor which they would claim." This delegate added that he was "not disposed to say that the masses of the people were all competent judges of a man's capacity as an expounder of one of the most abstruse sciences" or "admit that they were all competent to judge whether a man whom they never saw, had read a sufficient number of books upon law—whether he had the mind to understand what he had read—or was qualified with legal knowledge sufficient to discharge the duties of a judge." Finally, the delegate concluded with an analogy: "A man presented himself to the people as a candidate for the professorship of chemistry, would any one say that the masses of the people were competent to decide whether that man understood the science of chemistry, or [was] qualified to teach it?" (Cole 1919, 460).

The mid-nineteenth century sentiment that laypersons were not competent to evaluate judicial qualifications coincided with the cementation of legal formalism as the dominant theoretical perspective on judicial decision making (Horwitz 1975). According to the formalist perspective, law is largely determinate—even at the appellate level—and thus has a constraining effect on decision making, often leading judges to one "correct" case outcome. By the turn of the twentieth century, however, commitment to legal formalism began to break down both inside and outside the legal academy. Inside the legal academy, scholars condemned the notion of a "mechanical jurisprudence" (Pound 1908) with near deterministic decision making based on law. Instead, legal realists argued that law was indeterminate because legal texts such as constitutions and statutes, as well as generally agreed-on interpretive tools, often provided more than one plausible answer to contested legal questions. From this starting point, legal realists contended that observers must look to extralegal factors such as policy preferences or background characteristics to explain judicial decision making. Moreover, legal realists regularly declared explanations for reaching particular case outcomes to be little more than ad hoc rationalizations.

Outside the legal academy, political disenchantment intensified as elected judges were increasingly considered to be more committed to the political parties that ensured their election than the rule of law (see, e.g., Hanssen 2004). One delegate to the Ohio Constitutional Convention of 1912, for example, summarized mounting popular frustration with the perceived party influence over elections by declaring, "That the people have the power to and do select the judges is the veriest nonsense" (*Proceedings and Debates* 1912, 1052). This sentiment echoed predictions made by reform opposition delegates in New York more than a half century earlier. As frustration mounted, reformers disagreed about the best way to restore highly qualified, rather than merely partisan, judges to the bench. Some favored a return to an old institution while others called for experimentation.

Many newly organized state and local bar associations advocated for a return to judicial appointment to ensure a more qualified bench (see K. Hall 1984). However, Progressive reformers countered by suggesting a move to nonpartisan election in an effort to diminish the influence of political parties over judicial contests (Streb 2007, 10). In turn, several states adopted nonpartisan elections during the early part of the twentieth century. Critics, however, quickly suggested that nonpartisan elections only further diminished judicial talent in the states. Most prominently, departing president and later chief justice of the U.S. Supreme Court William Howard Taft (1913, 422) complained that with nonpartisan elections, candidates "are necessarily put in the attitude of supplicants before the people for preferment to judicial places," adding that "nothing could more impair the quality of lawyers available as candidates or depreciate the standard of the judiciary." Later, after several states implemented nonpartisan elections, the chair of the ABA's committee on judicial selection declared these elections a "failure" that "immersed the judges more deeply in politics, requiring each judge to build up his own political and publicity machine and even to give thought to the effect of his judicial decisions upon his political future" (J. Wood 1943, 142).

Early proponents of commission-based judicial selection plans emphasized the importance of selecting qualified judges even before those plans were labeled "merit selection." Albert Kales, who, as noted in Chapter 2, is generally credited with advancing the first commission-based selection plan, proclaimed that "the determination of who are qualified for [judicial] office is unusually difficult" (1914b, 232). In defense of his plan calling for a state's chief justice to make selections from a list forwarded by a commission of other judges, Kales emphasized what he perceived to be the judiciary's expertise and incentive to select candidates on the basis of qualifications: "No body of men in the state has a better opportunity for determining the character and ability of lawyers, since they examine the work of lawyers continually with most minute care" (239). When Harold Laski proposed a commission-based plan, with state supreme court justices, the state's attorney general, and the state bar association's president forming a group to provide the governor with judicial nominations, he argued that this committee of experts would be preferable to elections in part because of "the vital fact that the qualifications for judicial office are not such as an undifferentiated public can properly assess." Laski added that "[knowledge] of the law, the balanced mind, the ability to brush aside inessentials and drive to the heart of a case, that a candidate will possess these qualities can, at best, be known only to a few" (1926, 531). In the late 1930s, when the ABA officially called for commission-based judicial selection in the states, it suggested that "qualification alone" be the primary consideration and argued that a commission-based plan would succeed on this dimension, whereas other selection systems had failed (J. Wood 1938, 541).

Although the term "merit" had not yet been associated with commission-based judicial selection when Missouri became the first state to adopt such a system for supreme court justices in 1940, selecting more qualified judges was clearly among the chief goals advanced by reformers. Phrases like "merit system" and "merit selection" had been invoked, however, in the context of federal-level (Gailmard and Patty

2013) and state-level (Conover 1925) civil service reforms beginning in the late nineteenth century. The infusion of merit into discussions about government hiring grew out of frustration with the spoils system, which became pervasive following President Andrew Jackson's election in 1829. President James Garfield's assassination by an entitled job seeker turned away because of a lack of qualifications helped generate popular frustration with patronage-based appointments and played a role in creation of the nation's first merit-based hiring law—the Pendleton Civil Service Reform Act of 1883 (see Theriault 2003). Subsequently, Progressive Era reformers, who were also among the earliest proponents of commission-based judicial selection, pushed for broader reforms in government hiring based on merit and scientific management (Tolbert and Zucker 1983).

After it had long been referred to as the "American Bar Association Plan" or the "Missouri Plan," Nebraska State Bar Association president Laurens Williams appears to have been the first to publicly associate "merit" with commission-based judicial selection as early as 1953.[9] The American Judicature Society seems to have adopted the phrase "merit plan" to describe its commission-based judicial selection proposal by 1963 (Waterman 1963). After the American Judicature Society adopted the phrase "merit plan," it quickly spread in the legal literature, and commission-based plans throughout the country were referred to with this nomenclature. Indeed, after a decade of use in Nebraska but virtually nowhere else, one prominent judicial selection scholar noted that the phrase "merit plan" was "coming into general usage" less than three years after the American Judicature Society adopted the name (Winters 1966, 1085).

The popular association of "merit" with commission-based judicial selection seems to assume by definition that commission-based plans will generate a more highly qualified bench. However, the empirical evidence is mixed. Before detailing this literature, I distinguish three separate but sometimes overlapping research streams on judicial quality.[10] The first and perhaps best-developed stream analyzes the relationship between judicial retention mechanisms and judicial behavior. Specifically, this stream addresses whether variation in the level of independence afforded to judges influences their decision making on the bench. In salient cases, for example, judges who face competitive elections may be more inclined to decide cases in a way that pleases core constituencies (e.g., Brace and Boyea 2008; Melinda Gann Hall 1992, 1987).

A second stream analyzes the relationship between judicial selection institutions and judicial decision making. This research agenda has generated potentially important insights about merit selection. Damon Cann (2006), for example, finds that judges in states with merit selection rate the quality of their benches higher than judges in states with elections. Stephen Choi, Mitu Gulati, and Eric Posner (2010) find evidence that supreme court justices in states with merit selection are more productive than justices in states with other selection mechanisms but less independent; they find no difference between states with merit selection and other selection mechanisms with respect to the number of external citations to supreme court opinions. And supreme court decisions in states with merit selection are not more or less likely than others to be overturned by the U.S. Supreme Court (Owens et al. 2015).

Insofar as judicial selection and retention mechanisms coincide in some states, the first and second streams overlap. However, two complicating issues have received little attention. First, judicial selection and retention institutions are often distinct, as in merit plan states. Given that judicial selection and retention institutions may both be associated with judicial decision-making tendencies, it is important to distinguish the effects of each. This may be difficult when, as in merit selection states, the selection and retention mechanisms are strongly but not perfectly correlated.[11] Second, although judicial retention institutions operate at the state level, judicial selection institutions operate at the individual level in states that use a separate mechanism to fill interim vacancies. Most scholars have not accounted for the way that particular judges were seated when analyzing the relationship between judicial selection institutions and judicial behavior.

A third research stream, and the one this chapter contributes to, analyzes the link between judicial selection institutions and ex ante qualifications. Given that ex post judicial behavior may be endogenous to the operative retention mechanism, looking at ex ante qualifications offers a clear test of merit selection's impact. Moreover, examining the relationship between selection systems and judicial qualifications allows for the evaluation of core claims underlying the public policy debate over institutional design choices concerning judicial selection. Herbert Jacob (1964) collected background information on state trial court judges sitting in 1955 and found that those who were nominated by a commission were more likely to have obtained law school honors and less likely to have attended a "substandard" law school; commission-nominated trial court judges were also more likely to have prior judicial experience. However, Jacob noted that the results were "highly tentative" given the few merit appointments then in place, and it is not clear whether differences across systems were statistically significant (107). With a sample of 441 state supreme court justices, Bradley Canon (1972) found that a higher percentage of those put on the bench in gubernatorial appointment and legislative election states had prior judicial experience. However, as with Jacob's study, whether these differences were statistically significant is unclear. In the most systematic study of the relationship between selection systems and qualifications to date, Henry Glick and Craig Emmert (1987) used a sample of state supreme court justices serving in 1980 and 1981 and found that those who were appointed by governors (without a commission) were more likely to have attended elite law schools. With respect to previous judicial experience, however, Glick and Emmert found that "judges in all systems are similarly qualified for office" (233). A related study concluded that "no method of recruitment selects judges with substantially different credentials" (Emmert and Glick 1988, 445).

Empirical Analysis

To examine whether different judicial selection systems produce more or less qualified state supreme court justices, I use the database of state supreme court justices seated from 1960 through 2014, as described in Chapter 3 and Appendix A. Answering this question empirically requires objective information about judicial qualifications. Although some scholars have suggested that measuring ex ante qualifications is a fruitless endeavor, a wide array of stakeholders seem to consider several objective proxies relevant. The next part develops several measures of judicial qualifications across two categories: (1) law school quality and performance and (2) judicial experience.

Dependent Variables

Law school quality is commonly used to capture judicial qualifications. Having attended a quality law school can serve as a proxy for intelligence and learnedness in law.[12] Although judgments about law school quality are necessarily subjective to some extent, the influential *U.S. News and World Report* rankings offer the most consistent proxy for law school quality over time. Unfortunately, these rankings did not begin until 1987, were not issued yearly until 1990, and did not rank more than twenty-five law schools until 1992.[13] Less than 2 percent of seating events in the sample took place in 1992 or later. Following Maya Sen (2014), who used a single year's *U.S. News and World Report* law school rankings to capture qualifications for federal judges seated across several decades, I use a single year's rankings to capture qualifications for state supreme court justices.[14] As Sen notes, this results in "a somewhat rough measure for judges [who graduated from law school in other years, but] an assuaging factor is that the composition of the top 14 schools has not changed over time" (41). Indeed, law school reputation more broadly is fairly stable over time (see Schmalbeck 1998). Notwithstanding considerable controversy over the methodology *U.S. News and World Report* employs to generate its rankings, they are widely considered a useful coordination mechanism for sorting the most talented students into schools offering the best education (see Korobkin 1998).

I use three measures of law school quality. Whether a justice attended an elite law school is perhaps the most common measure of law school quality (e.g., Bonneau 2001; Glick and Emmert 1987). Although the elite law school concept can be operationalized in different ways, the least arbitrary and most consistent measure is whether a law school is among the top-fourteen (T14) law schools in the *U.S. News and World Report*'s law school rankings (see also Bonica, Chilton, and Sen 2014; Hinkle et al. 2012; M. Nelson 2014).[15] Although rankings within the T14 differ somewhat from year to year, the T14 schools have been stable over time (Henderson 2013, 65; Sen 2014, 41).[16] Following Sen (2014, 41), the second measure of law school quality takes into account gradations beyond the T14 threshold. Specifically, this measure is an ordered variable increasing in quality with the following categories: (1) schools not ranked in the top one hundred, (2) schools ranked one hundred through seventy-six, (3) schools ranked seventy-five through fifty-one, (4) schools ranked fifty through twenty-six, (5) schools ranked twenty-five through fifteen, and (6) T14 schools.[17] Of course, many very good students attend in-state institutions even if they are not among the most prestigious law schools. Common reasons for this decision include a desire to be close to family, pay in-state tuition at public schools, and work in-state after graduation. For a more localized measure of law school quality, I created an indicator scored one if one of the following conditions was met and zero otherwise: (1) the judge graduated from a T14 school, (2) the judge graduated from the state's flagship public law school, or (3) the judge graduated from an in-state law school ranked higher than the state's flagship law school.[18]

Although employing law school quality to measure qualifications is common and informative, it has been criticized for not taking academic performance into account (W. Smith 2010, 672). A top-performing student from a lower-ranked law school, for example, may be considered more meritorious postgraduation than a middling student from a better law school. In addition to signaling legal expertise, academic performance serves as a proxy for intelligence—long considered an important factor in judicial selection decisions (see, e.g., Charles, Chen, and Gulati 2011). The existing literature on state judicial selection does not account for academic performance, perhaps because it is difficult to capture empirically. Law school transcripts are not publicly available, and having graduated with honors is not regularly mentioned in typically sparse biographical materials. As a result, not uncovering evidence that justices graduated with honors does not necessarily mean that they did not graduate with honors.

I overcome these difficulties with an objective measure of academic performance that can be obtained using publicly available information: service on a law school's primary law review.[19] Law review membership, which is typically based on grades, performance in a write-on competition, or some combination of these factors, is widely considered to be a valuable educational experience in addition to being one of the most important honors bestowed on law students and a credible sign of academic ability (Cane 1981). Not only do "the best students" serve on law review, but membership has been an important signal in legal circles for more than a century (Peppers 2006, 30). As a result, scholars have employed law review membership to tap into academic performance (see also Szmer and Ginn 2014).[20]

Notwithstanding that law review membership may be a somewhat obscure qualification for most laypersons, it is regularly emphasized in the political arena. Judgeship applications in Montana, for example, specifically ask whether the applicant was a member of law review.[21] Moreover, judges, governors, and presidents regularly cite law review membership as a judicial qualification. Texas Supreme Court justice Phil Johnson's website notes, for example, that "he attended Texas Tech University School of Law, where he was a member of the law review" ("About," n.d.). When Kansas governor Sam Brownback nominated Caleb Stegall to the Kansas Court of Appeals, a few months before nominating him to the Kansas Supreme Court, he praised Stegall's "academic accomplishment" while specifically mentioning that "he served as a member of the Kansas Law Review" ("Introductory Comments," n.d.). And when President Bill Clinton nominated Ruth Bader Ginsburg to fill a vacancy on the U.S. Supreme Court he emphasized that she had "served on the law reviews [at both Harvard and Columbia]" (Clinton 1993).[22] The law review indicator is scored one if a justice served on law review and zero otherwise.

Judicial experience is the second category of qualifications considered here. Indeed, prior judicial experience is the most frequently cited indicator of qualifications for service on the nation's highest appellate benches. At the federal level, prior judicial experience is considered "a near prerequisite" for appointment to the U.S. Supreme Court (Epstein, Knight, and Martin 2003, 906). At the state level, scholars have used prior judicial experience as a measure of candidate quality (e.g., Bonneau and Cann 2011; Bonneau and Hall 2003; Hall and Bonneau 2006). Previous studies of judicial selection systems and qualifications have also emphasized prior judicial experience, noting that it speaks to the existence of "superior judicial credentials" (Glick and Emmert 1987, 233). Furthermore, public opinion data suggest that previous judicial experience is the most important qualification for obtaining appellate judgeships (Barnes and Agiesta 2010).

I use four measures of judicial experience. First, I created an indicator variable scored one for state supreme court justices who had previous judicial experience and zero otherwise. Second, I created a variable counting the number of years the justice served as a judge before being seated. This variable accounts for someone with, say, twenty years of judicial experience possibly being considered more qualified than someone with one year of judicial experience. Third, I created an indicator variable scored one for state supreme court justices with previous appellate judicial experience and zero otherwise. Although several states do not have intermediate appellate courts, and thus are not included in this analysis, appellate judges in states that have these courts may be considered more qualified for state supreme court vacancies (cf. Bonneau and Hall 2009, 101). At the federal level, for example, individuals with appellate experience have filled the overwhelming majority of recent U.S. Supreme Court vacancies. Last, I created a variable counting the number of years of appellate experience for justices seated in states with intermediate appellate courts. Given the difficulty of determining how many years individuals served on the bench before being seated on their state supreme courts going back in time, the years of experience models include justices seated from 2000 through 2014.

Figure 4.1 plots summary information for each of the previously described dependent variables. The first panel plots the percentage of seatings of a justice with each binary qualification.[23] Having graduated from an elite law school is the least common of these qualifications (22 percent of seatings), followed by having served on law review (25 percent of seatings), having appellate experience (28 percent of seatings), having attended a locally elite law school (61 percent of seatings), and having some judicial experience (68 percent of seatings). Panel 2 plots seatings across the six categories included in the ordered law school rankings. Law schools ranked below the top one hundred were represented in 22 percent of seatings, schools ranked seventy-six to one hundred in 11 percent of seatings, schools ranked fifty-one to seventy-five in 13 percent of seatings, schools ranked twenty-six to fifty in 20 percent of seatings, schools ranked fifteen to twenty-five in 11 percent of seatings, and T14 schools in 22 percent of seatings.[24]

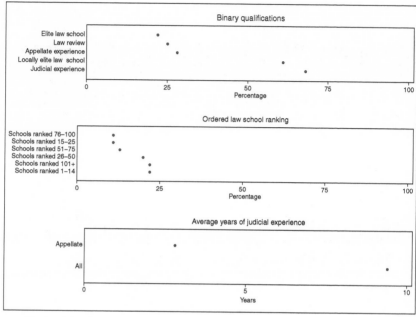

Figure 4.1 Summary statistics: qualifications

Last, Panel 3 plots the average total years of any judicial experience (nine) and appellate experience (three) for seatings in this sample.

Independent Variables

There are two key explanatory variables. The appointment variable is scored one for justices who were seated by elite appointment and zero otherwise. The election variable is scored one for justices who were seated through partisan or nonpartisan election and zero otherwise. Merit selection is the excluded baseline. Figures 4.2–4.4, respectively, plot summary statistics across selection systems for the binary, ordered law school ranking, and average years of judicial experience dependent variables. In addition to the key explanatory variables, several control variables, described in greater detail in Chapter 3, are included: a measure of court professionalism, court size, term years, mandatory retirement, the natural log of the number of lawyers in a state, and state

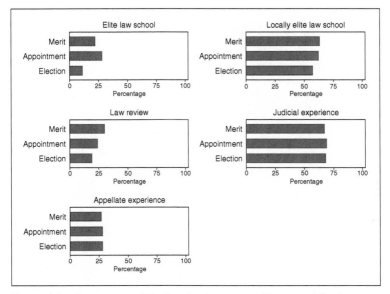

Figure 4.2 Summary statistics by selection system: binary qualifications

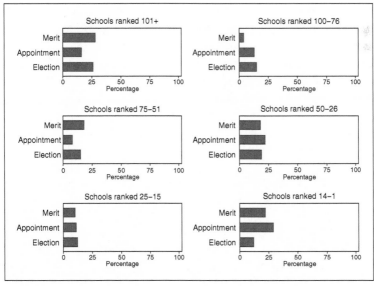

Figure 4.3 Summary statistics by selection system: ordered law school ranking

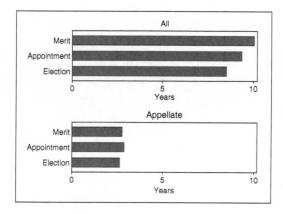

Figure 4.4
Summary statistics by selection system: average years of judicial experience

liberalism. The models also include region fixed effects, and those estimated over the entire sample period include a cubic polynomial approximation to account for temporal dynamics.

Analysis and Results

The models with binary dependent variables are fit with logistic regression, the ordered law school quality model is fit with ordinal logistic regression, and the years of experience models are fit with negative binomial regression.[25] Standard errors are clustered by state to account for nonindependence within states. In each model, the qualification measure used as the dependent variable is coded moving from less to more qualified.

For interested readers, Tables B3 and B4 in Appendix B display the complete multivariate results for each model.[26] Although the estimated coefficients and standard errors in these tables provide information about statistical significance, they do not convey readily interpretable information about substantive impact. To provide easy-to-interpret information about substantive differences across selection systems, Table 4.1 presents changes in quantities of interest (predicted probabilities or expected counts depending on the model) associated with seating qualified justices moving from the first selection institution to the second.[27] Table 4.1 also includes 95 percent confidence intervals

TABLE 4.1   CHANGE IN QUANTITIES OF INTEREST: QUALIFICATIONS

	Merit vs. appointment	Merit vs. election	Appointment vs. election
Binary qualifications (predicted probabilities)			
Elite law school	4% (–3%, 11%)	–6%* (–12%, –1%)	–10%* (–15%, –4%)
Locally elite law school	–3% (–5%, 11%)	≈0 (–9%, 9%)	–3% (–11%, 4%)
Law review	–3% (–10%, 4%)	–8%* (–15%, –1%)	–5% (–11%, 2%)
Any judicial experience	–3% (–12%, 6%)	–2% (–13%, 9%)	1% (–8%, 10%)
Appellate experience	≈0% (–5%, 6%)	≈0% (–7%, 8%)	≈0% (–6%, 6%)
Ordered rankings (predicted probabilities)			
Law school ranked 101+	–1% (–7%, 5%)	5% (–1%, 11%)	6%* (2%, 11%)
Law school ranked 76–100	–1% (–3%, 2%)	2% (–1%, 4%)	2%* (1%, 4%)
Law school ranked 51–75	≈0% (–2%, 2%)	1% (–1%, 3%)	2% (–1%, 3%)
Law school ranked 26–50	≈0% (–1%, 1%)	–1% (–2%, 1%)	–1% (–2%, 1%)
Law school ranked 15–25	≈0% (–2%, 3%)	–2% (–4%, 1%)	–2%* (–4%, –1%)
Law school ranked 1–14	2% (–6%, 10%)	–5% (–12%, 2%)	–7%* (–12%, –2%)
Judicial experience (expected years)			
Any	–3 (–6, 1)	–3 (–6, <1)	≈0 (–3, 3)
Appellate	–2 (–4, 1)	–2 (–4, 1)	≈0 (–1, 2)

Note: Numbers outside parentheses are changes in predicted probabilities or expected counts moving from the first selection system to the second. Parentheses contain 95 percent confidence intervals. Results from the full models that generated these results are presented in Tables B3 and B4 in Appendix B.

*$p < 0.05$ (two-tailed).

around the predicted change in probability, indicating whether the difference is statistically distinguishable from zero at that threshold.

As with professional experience, state supreme court justices seated across selection systems have more similarities than differences in their judicial qualifications. Indeed, none of the differences across pairwise selection system comparisons are statistically distinguishable from zero for any of the judicial experience measures: having any judicial experience, having appellate judicial experience (in states with intermediate appellate courts), years served as a judge, and years served as an appellate judge (in states with intermediate appellate courts). These results are particularly notable because of the emphasis many stakeholders place on the importance of previous judicial experience in determining whether someone is qualified to fill a high court vacancy.

While there are more similarities than differences in terms of law school quality and performance across selection systems, several results are worth noting. State supreme court justices seated by election are less likely than justices seated through merit selection or appointment to have attended an elite law school. Substantively, the probability of seating a justice who attended an elite law school decreases from 18 percent (95 percent confidence interval of 13 percent, 23 percent) under merit selection to 12 percent (9 percent, 16 percent) under election, a change of –6 percent (–12 percent, –1 percent). The probability of seating a justice who attended an elite law school decreases from 22 percent (16 percent, 28 percent) under appointment to 12 percent (9 percent, 16 percent) under election, a change of –10 percent (–15 percent, –4 percent). With respect to academic performance, the probability of seating a justice who served on law review decreases from 28 percent (22 percent, 34 percent) to 20 percent (15 percent, 25 percent) under merit selection, a change of –8 percent (–15 percent, –1 percent). Using the locally elite law school measure, none of the differences between selection systems are statistically distinguishable from zero.

Turning to the ordinal law school rankings, differences between merit selection and appointment and differences between merit selection and election are not statistically distinguishable from zero. However, there are several notable differences between appointment and election.[28] State supreme court justices seated by election are more likely to have graduated from a law school ranked in the bottom two categories compared to justices seated by appointment. Moreover, justices seated by election are less likely to have graduated from a law school ranked in the top two categories compared to justices seated by appointment. Substantively, the probability of seating under appointment versus election a justice who attended a school ranked lower than the top one hundred increases from 16 percent (10 percent, 21 percent) to 22 percent (14 percent, 29 percent), a change of 6 percent (2 percent, 11 percent); ranked seventy-six to one hundred increases from 10 percent (4 percent, 16 percent) to 12 percent (5 percent, 19 percent), a change of 2 percent (1 percent, 4 percent); ranked fifteen to twenty-five decreases from 14 percent (8 percent, 19 percent) to 12 percent (6 percent, 16 percent), a change of –2 percent (–4 percent, –1 percent); or ranked in the T14 decreases from 25 percent (18 percent, 32 percent) to 18 percent (14 percent, 22 percent), a change of –7 percent (–12 percent, –2 percent).

None of the control variables are consistent predictors of state supreme court justices being seated with particular qualifications. In the ordered law school rankings model, increasing court professionalism from one standard deviation below its mean to one standard deviation above is associated with a decrease in the probability of seating a justice who graduated from a law school ranked lower than the top one hundred from 18 percent (11 percent, 24 percent) to 13 percent (8 percent, 19 percent), a change of –5 percent (–9 percent, –1 percent). The same increase in professionalism is associated with an increase in the probability of seating a justice who graduated from a T14 law school from 22 percent (15 percent, 30 percent) to 29 percent (22 percent, 36 percent), a change of 7 percent (1 percent, 13 percent). That increase in court professionalism is associated with a decrease in the probability of seating a justice who graduated from a locally elite law school from 69 percent (64 percent, 75 percent) to 60 percent (54 percent, 67 percent), a change of –9 percent (–14 percent, –4 percent). The same increase in court professionalism is also associated with an increase in the expected number of years serving as an intermediate appellate judge (for those states with intermediate appellate courts) from two (one, three) to three (two, five), a change of one (one, three). Overall, these results provide mixed evidence on the relationship between court professionalism and seating qualified state supreme court justices. Court size also yields mixed results on different measures of qualifications. Increasing court size from its minimum (three) to maximum (nine) value is associated with a decrease in the probability of seating a justice who attended a locally elite law school from 73 percent (64 percent, 83 percent) to 56 percent (48 percent, 65 percent), a change of –17 percent (–31 percent, –3 percent). However, the same increase in court size is associated with an increase in the probability of seating a justice with appellate experience from 20 percent (12 percent, 27 percent) to 31 percent (24 percent, 37 percent), a change of 11 percent (1 percent, 21 percent).

Conclusion

The core question underlying the contemporary merit selection debate is whether it yields better-qualified judges on average than other selection systems. As the historical evidence presented in this chapter demonstrates, however, the question of which selection institution produces the best-qualified judges is not new. Indeed, stakeholders have invoked claims about the link between selection systems and judicial qualifications at every turn during America's long-running debate over the optimal method of selecting judges. Notwithstanding the debate's endurance, efforts to evaluate comparative institutional performance with respect to producing qualified state supreme court justices have stalled because of methodological limitations. As a result, participants in this debate have been left to speculate about each selection system's ability to yield qualified state supreme court justices.

Using new data that improve on the limitations inherent in existing studies, the results presented here offer the most comprehensive analysis of the relationship between judicial selection institutions and qualifications to date. Overall, the results suggest that no selection system enjoys a systematic advantage over any other system. Merit selection and appointment performed similarly across each measure of qualifications. In terms of judicial experience, regardless of how it is measured, each of the three major judicial selection systems seems to produce justices with similar qualifications. There were, however, several differences across institutional settings with respect to law school quality and performance. Merit selection outperformed election with respect to academic performance, and appointment outperformed election on certain measures of law school quality.

Careful consideration of two issues is required before determining how these results should influence the debate over choice of judicial selection institutions. As an initial matter, reasonable observers can disagree about the relative weight to afford the specific qualifications analyzed here. Second, although one of the benefits of the approach employed here is that it leverages objective and well-accepted measures of judicial qualifications, few if any would contend that these measures constitute the universe of relevant qualifications. Certainly, difficult-to-measure qualifications such as temperament, integrity, and virtue may be important factors when making judicial selection decisions (see Solum 2005). And it is possible that one selection system does a better job sorting on these characteristics than other systems. However, with respect to readily measurable qualifications that are regularly invoked in contemporary judicial selection debates, no selection system consistently outperforms the others.

5 | Seating Diverse Justices

Does merit selection yield a more diverse judiciary? While the debate over merit selection has long emphasized qualifications, recent decades have seen stakeholders increasingly making claims about its impact on diversity. Near the end of the twentieth century, for example, one prominent proponent stated that "merit selection is a time-tested process that results in a well-qualified judiciary and increases diversity on the bench" (Brown 1996, 53). Indeed, it is now a common refrain among proponents to suggest that merit selection increases judicial diversity (see, e.g., Bierman 2002, 856; Caufield 2010, 781–784; Zeidman 2005, 721; Fund for Modern Courts, n.d.; League of Women Voters of Hawaii 2003; League of Women Voters of Illinois 2014, 12–15). Just as merit selection is said to increase the overall quality of the judiciary by deemphasizing political connections and pressures, advocates have suggested that this depoliticization should increase diversity by removing institutionally imposed favoritism for long-entrenched majority interests. Others, however, have suggested that merit selection hinders judicial diversity. Former U.S. senator and then-gubernatorial candidate Roland Burris proclaimed that he did "not support merit selection because it's not fair to minorities" ("Changing" 2002). These competing claims persist in part because the empirical literature has not rendered definitive answers about the relationship between judicial selection institutions and judicial diversity. One scholar, for example, summarizes the state of the literature by suggesting that "existing studies have produced vastly different results about the effects of judicial selection systems regarding gender and racial diversity in state courts" (K. Myers 2013, 48).

In this chapter, I use new data to reexamine the question of whether certain judicial selection institutions are more or less likely to produce diverse state supreme court justices. In addition to answering an important question concerning comparative institutional performance, the study of judicial diversification has significant social implications. As an initial matter, the study of descriptive representation focuses on the consequences of alignment between the characteristics of officeholders and those they represent (Pitkin 1967). The literature on descriptive representation in political institutions suggests that it may have beneficial consequences, such as increasing trust, knowledge, participation, and institutional legitimacy (e.g., Bobo and Gilliam 1990; Gay 2002; Mansbridge 1999). In one study of race and descriptive representation in the judiciary, for example, blacks indicated more support for courts as the number of black judges serving on those courts increased (Scherer and Curry 2010). Although the literature on gender and descriptive representation yields mixed results (e.g., Broockman 2014; Reingold and Harrell 2010; Wolak 2014), there is evidence that female representation in a political institution increases women's political knowledge of that institution and willingness to engage in political activity (Fridkin and Kenney 2014). While there is little empirical evidence regarding the effects of gender diversity in the judiciary, anecdotal accounts suggest that many judges support the goal of descriptive representation on the understanding that it improves judicial legitimacy (see Scherer 2011, 601–604).[1]

In contrast to descriptive representation, substantive representation emphasizes the extent to which a representative's actions reflect group preferences (Pitkin 1967). For example, there is evidence that black federal appellate court judges are more likely to vote to uphold affirmative action programs; furthermore, white judges are more likely to uphold affirmative action programs when randomly assigned to a panel with a black judge (Kastellec 2013).[2] Although there appears to be little systematic difference between the way that male and female judges decide cases across issue areas, female judges are more likely than males to support plaintiffs in gender discrimination cases; furthermore, male judges are more likely to support plaintiffs in gender discrimination cases when a female judge is randomly assigned to the panel (Boyd, Epstein, and Martin 2010).[3] In the states, one study found that nonwhite state supreme court justices on courts with discretionary jurisdiction were more likely than white justices to vote to overturn criminal convictions (Bonneau and Rice 2009).

The presence of political minorities on the bench can influence judicial decision making in ways other than voting. One study found that while white and nonwhite judges voted similarly in cases involving criminal sentencing guidelines, nonwhite judges were more likely "to adopt a nonmainstream approach" or "experiment with alternative theories" (Sisk, Heise, and Morriss 1998, 1459). And survey evidence suggests that women bring different experiences and perspectives to the bench than their male counterparts (Martin 1990). Even if gender differences do not manifest themselves in different voting patterns, they may nonetheless be important (see, generally, Kenney 2013). On a collegial court, for example, the random assignment of a female judge changes the way that opinions are written across a variety of substantive issue areas (Gill and Hall 2015).[4] Furthermore, one study found that female state supreme court justices were more likely than their male counterparts to demonstrate political independence by dissenting more often from opinions written by copartisans (Choi et al. 2011).[5]

This chapter contributes to the literatures on judicial selection and diversity in several ways. First, I trace the historical development of the push toward gender and racial diversification of the judiciary. This historical and political context helps explain why judicial diversity, unlike qualifications, was not at the forefront of early arguments concerning merit selection or, for that matter, any of the early debates about judicial selection institutions. In short, formal and informal barriers protracted the push toward professional equality. As these barriers cracked, and political momentum for institutional diversity developed during the last quarter of the twentieth century, questions increasingly arose about the connection between selection systems and judicial diversification. Second, I explain how arguments linking merit selection with increased judicial diversification became more popular during President Jimmy Carter's push for a different type of merit selection at the federal level. After developing this political and historical context, I offer an overview of the existing literature on the relationship between selection systems and judicial diversification with an eye toward illuminating this chapter's empirical contribution. Although some have concluded that there is no relationship between selection mechanisms and judicial diversification, the results presented here are more nuanced. While no selection system consistently outperforms all others across categories, there are important differences across institutions.

Diversifying Courts

Women Judges

When women began seeking formal access to the legal profession in larger numbers during the late 1860s, they encountered formidable formal and informal barriers to professional equality. At common law, "the very being or legal existence of the woman is suspended during the marriage, or at least is incorporated and consolidated into that of the husband: under whose wing, protection, and cover, she performs every thing; and is therefore called in our law-french a feme-covert; is said to be covert-baron, or under the protection and influence of her husband, her baron, or lord" (Blackstone 1759, 430). Specific common law rules held that "a married woman could not enter contracts, hold or convey property, retain her own earnings, bring legal actions, or acquire a passport based on her own nationality" (O'Connor 1996, 658). Moreover, married and unmarried women faced legal prohibitions against voting, holding public office, serving on a jury, and becoming a notary public (658).

The rise of a coordinated women's movement along with increasing industrialization during the middle of the nineteenth century helped generate legal reforms that began eroding the doctrine of coverture and granting married women certain contractual and property rights (see, e.g., Shammas 1994). Although the U.S. Supreme Court declared that the "institution of coverture is peculiar and obsolete" a century later (*United States v. Yazell* 1966, 350), vestiges of women's subordination to men under the law remain to this day (see, e.g., Hasday 2000), and formal legal barriers to women's equality remained staunch well into the twentieth century. As part of the social change that began with the women's movement in the middle of the nineteenth century (see, e.g., DuBois 1978; Ryan 1992), women increasingly sought access to the legal profession. The nation's first female law students were admitted in the late 1860s (Norgren 2013, 35–36). Arabella Mansfield became the first woman admitted to a state bar association when Iowa admitted her in 1869 (Weisberg 1977, 485). One year later, Ada Kepley graduated from the Union College of Law of the Old University of Chicago (now Northwestern University), becoming the first woman to earn a law degree (485). Kepley, however, was denied admission to the Illinois bar because women were not permitted to be members.[6]

The state's decision to deny women bar membership played out just before Kepley's graduation and ultimately led to a U.S. Supreme Court decision that provides an illustrative look into the era's lack of formal legal protections concerning gender equality. After serving as an apprentice to enter the legal profession, a common route to practicing law at the time, Myra Bradwell "passed the Illinois Bar Exam with high honors" in 1869 and applied for admission to the Illinois bar (J. Friedman 1993, 17–18). Subsequently, the Illinois Supreme Court directed the court reporter to deny her application "upon the ground that [she] would not be bound by the obligations necessary to be assumed where the relation of attorney and client shall exist, by reason of the disability imposed by [her] married condition—it being assumed that [she is] a married woman" (Lupton 2011, 240). Bradwell then sued the state of Illinois, alleging that its refusal to grant bar admission violated the Fourteenth Amendment's Privileges or Immunities Clause.[7] Deciding the case in 1873, shortly after nearly eviscerating the Privileges or Immunities Clause in the *Slaughter-House Cases* (1873), the U.S. Supreme Court voted 8–1 to reject Bradwell's constitutional claim (*Bradwell v. Illinois* 1873). Although Justice Samuel Freeman Miller's majority opinion emphasized the Court's view that the ability to practice law was not protected by the Fourteenth Amendment's Privileges or Immunities Clause, Justice Joseph Bradley's concurrence, joined by Justices Noah Haynes Swayne and Stephen Johnson Field, offered a glimpse into political and social attitudes regarding women's involvement in the legal profession at the time. Bradley wrote:

> The civil law, as well as nature herself, has always recognized a wide difference in the respective spheres and destinies of man and woman. Man is, or should be, woman's protector and defender. The natural and proper timidity and delicacy which belongs to the female gender evidently unfits it for many of the occupations of civil life. The constitution of the family organization, which is founded in the divine ordinance, as well as in the nature of things, indicates the domestic sphere as that which properly belongs to the domain and functions of womanhood. The harmony, not to say identity, of interests and views which belong, or should belong, to the family institution is repugnant to the idea of a woman adopting a distinct and independent career from that of her husband. (*Bradwell v. Illinois* 1873, 141)

Justice Bradley's position was not an aberration during this era. In response to Lavina Goodell's application for admission to the Wisconsin bar, for example, the Wisconsin Supreme Court declared, "The law of nature destines and qualifies the female gender for the bearing and nurture of the children of our race and for the custody of the homes of the world and their maintenance in love and honor. And all life-long callings of women, inconsistent with these radical and sacred duties of their gender, as is the profession of the law, are departures from the order of nature; and when voluntary, treason against it" (*In re Goodell* 1875, 244). The Court continued, "There are many employments in life not unfit for female character. The profession of the law is surely not one of these. The peculiar qualities of womanhood, its gentle graces, its quick sensibility, its tender susceptibility, its purity, its delicacy, its emotional impulses, its subordination of hard reason to sympathetic feeling, are surely not qualifications for forensic strife. Nature has tempered woman as little for the juridical conflicts of the court room, as for the physical conflicts of the battle field. Womanhood is moulded for gentler and better things" (245–246).[8]

Notwithstanding the series of important firsts regarding women in the law that occurred during the late nineteenth century, the struggle for social, political, and professional equality continued. From the middle of the nineteenth century, social and political momentum slowly developed toward women's suffrage, which was eventually enshrined in the U.S. Constitution in 1920 by the Nineteenth Amendment. Little changed in the ensuing decades, however, with respect to women's advancement in the legal profession. As an initial matter, facial discrimination against women in the workplace remained embedded in the law. In 1948, for example, the U.S. Supreme Court upheld a Michigan law refusing to award licenses to sell alcohol to a woman unless she was "the wife or daughter of the male owner" (*Goesaert v. Cleary* 1948, 465, quoting the Public Acts of Michigan). Although the Fourteenth Amendment's Equal Protection Clause prohibits states from "deny[ing] to any person within its jurisdiction the equal protection of the laws," Justice Frankfurter wrote for a 6–3 majority that "the fact that women may now have achieved the virtues that men have long claimed as their prerogatives and now indulge in vices that men have long practiced, does not preclude the States from drawing a sharp line between the sexes, certainly in such matters as the regulation of the liquor traffic" (466).

Informal discrimination persisted alongside the formal discrimination embedded in law. U.S. Supreme Court Justice Ruth Bader Ginsburg (2004, 803) once noted, for example, that "the few women who braved law school in the 1950s and 1960s, it was generally supposed, presented no real challenge to (or competition for) the men." This mind-set is captured by an anecdote concerning Chief Justice William Rehnquist and Justice Sandra Day O'Connor. Although both were appointed to the U.S. Supreme Court, their paths were markedly different: both graduated at the top of their Stanford law class in 1952, at which point Rehnquist secured a prestigious U.S. Supreme Court clerkship with Justice Robert H. Jackson, while O'Connor failed to secure a single paid offer as an attorney.[9] At O'Connor's lone interview with a law firm, a partner said he might be able to secure her a legal secretary position if she could type well enough but added, "We have never hired a woman as a lawyer here, and I don't see the time when we will" (Greenburg 2007, 10, quoting O'Connor). Eventually, O'Connor secured a nonpaying position with the San Mateo district attorney's office before being elevated to a paid position as a deputy district attorney (L. Myers 2007, 6). After moving from California to Arizona in 1957, O'Connor once again failed to secure an offer from a law firm and started a small practice with another attorney (O'Connor 2001, 1).

During the early 1960s and into the 1970s, a renewed women's movement actively lobbied for reform and laws were enacted to address issues concerning gender discrimination. The Equal Pay Act of 1963 and Civil Rights Act of 1964 were major legal reforms enacted in part to address gender discrimination, respectively prohibiting gender-based wage differentials and workplace discrimination by covered employers (see Kanowitz 1968). In 1972, Congress proposed the Equal Rights Amendment (ERA), which stipulated that "equality of rights under the law shall not be denied or abridged by the United States or by any State on account of gender."[10] One estimate suggested that the ERA would have brought into question the validity of "over 800 provisions" of federal law containing gender-based classifications (Ginsburg 1978, 22). Although the ERA fell short of ratification (see Mansbridge 1986), several states passed versions that resulted in state courts applying a higher level of scrutiny to gender-based classifications (Baldez, Epstein, and Martin 2006). This resulted in many gender-based classifications being invalidated.

At the federal level, the U.S. Supreme Court invalidated its first gender-based classification under the Fourteenth Amendment's Equal Protection Clause in 1971. In *Reed v. Reed* (1971), the Court invalidated an Idaho law declaring that "males must be preferred to females" as choices to administer an estate when there were two members of a class (e.g., parents) seeking administrative power. Following *Reed*, the Court signaled its commitment to prohibiting certain gender-based classifications under the Fourteenth Amendment's Equal Protection Clause by invalidating several state and federal laws. In *Frontiero v. Richardson* (1973), for example, the Court invalidated a federal law allowing servicemen to claim their wives as dependents for benefits purposes even if their wives were not actually dependent while requiring servicewomen to demonstrate that their husbands were in fact dependent to obtain the same benefits. And in *Stanton v. Stanton* (1975), the Court invalidated a Utah law that required financial support for male children until the age of twenty-one and females until the age of eighteen.

Although cases like *Reed*, *Frontiero*, and *Stanton* signaled that the Court was willing to invalidate certain gender-based classifications as violations of the Fourteenth Amendment's Equal Protection Clause, the Court had been unable to agree on a generally applicable legal standard to apply in other cases until 1976. In *Craig v. Boren* (1976), the Court invalidated an Oklahoma law permitting the sale of 3.2 percent beer to males under the age of twenty-one and females under the age of eighteen. In doing so, the Court announced that "to withstand constitutional challenge . . . classifications by gender must serve important governmental objectives and must be substantially related to achievement of those objectives" (197). This rule replaced a more lenient one that required only that a gender-based classification "must be reasonable, not arbitrary, and must rest upon some ground of difference having a fair and substantial relation to the object of the legislation" (*Reed v. Reed* 1971, 76, quoting *Royster Guano Co. v. Virginia* 1920, 415).[11] As a result of these jurisprudential developments, the Fourteenth Amendment's Equal Protection Clause became an important tool for eradicating gender-based classifications embedded in state and federal law.[12]

Gender diversification of the federal judiciary began in 1934, when Florence Ellinwood Allen became the first female judge on an Article III court after President Franklin D. Roosevelt nominated her to the U.S. Court of Appeals for the Sixth Circuit (Cedarbaum 1993, 40).[13] After Allen's landmark confirmation, fifteen years passed before Burnita Shelton Matthews became the second woman seated on an Article III court—and the first to be seated as a district judge—after President Harry Truman nominated her to the U.S. District Court for the District of Columbia in 1949 (Ginsburg and Brill 1995, 284). Following her service as an assistant state attorney general, state senator, state trial court judge, and state appellate court judge, Sandra Day O'Connor became the first female U.S. Supreme Court justice in 1981 when President Reagan fulfilled a campaign promise to nominate the first woman to the bench (Maveety 1996, 14–15). As of 2015, three additional women have been appointed to the U.S. Supreme Court: Ruth Bader Ginsburg (nominated by President Clinton in 1993), Sonia

Sotomayor (nominated by President Obama in 2009), and Elena Kagan (nominated by President Obama in 2010).

As at the federal level, the pace of gender diversification on state courts proceeded slowly (see Goelzhauser 2011). Shortly after the Nineteenth Amendment's ratification, Florence Ellinwood Allen, who, as previously noted, would become the first female Article III judge, became the first female state supreme court justice upon election to the Ohio Supreme Court in 1922 (Ginsburg and Brill 1995, 282–283).[14] Although the Nineteenth Amendment's ratification helped spur the diversification of political institutions more generally, thirty-seven years passed following Allen's 1922 election before Rhoda Valentine Lewis (Hawaii) and Jennie Loitman Barron (Massachusetts) became the next female state supreme court justices seated in 1959. Only two other states seated their first female supreme court justices in the 1960s. Beginning in the second half of the 1970s, states slowly diversified their supreme courts by seating their first female justices. South Dakota became the last state to seat its first female supreme court justice in 2002.

Black Judges

Antebellum America witnessed little gender or racial integration of the legal profession, much less the judiciary. In *Dred Scott v. Sandford* (1857, 404), the U.S. Supreme Court held that blacks "are not included, and were not intended to be included, under the word 'citizens' in the Constitution, and can therefore claim none of the rights and privileges which that instrument provides for and secures to citizens of the United States." Chief Justice Roger B. Taney went on to summarize the contemporary state of political and legal affairs, noting that blacks "had for more than a century before been regarded as beings of an inferior order, and altogether unfit to associate with the white race, either in social or political relations; and so far inferior, that they had no rights which the white man was bound to respect; and that the negro might justly and lawfully be reduced to slavery for his benefit" (407).

Although the Reconstruction Amendments eliminated certain formal legal barriers for blacks in the years following the Civil War, Jim Crow laws quickly filled in gaps to ensure continuing segregation and barriers to social, political, and legal equality.[15] The barriers to a legal education created by segregation proved particularly formidable at limiting professional access. In *Plessy v. Ferguson* (1896, 544), the U.S. Supreme Court upheld the constitutionality of segregated train cars by a 7–1 vote, declaring that the Fourteenth Amendment's Equal Protection Clause "was undoubtedly to enforce the absolute equality of the two races before the law, but in the nature of things it could not have been intended to abolish distinctions based upon color, or to enforce social, as distinguished from political equality, or a commingling of the two races upon terms unsatisfactory to either."[16] *Plessy*'s lone dissenting opinion may provide an even clearer signal of the glacial progress toward full equality in more than thirty years following the Civil War. Although Justice John Marshall Harlan's dissent is often cited for its forward-looking position that the "Constitution is color-blind, and neither knows nor tolerates classes among citizens," it is important to note that he was contrasting legal and social equality; on the latter, Harlan wrote, "The white race deems itself to be the dominant race in this country. And so it is, in prestige, in achievements, in education, in wealth and in power. So, I doubt not, it will continue to be for all time, if it remains true to its great heritage and holds fast to the principles of constitutional liberty" (559).

The process of incorporating black males into the legal profession began before the Civil War. In 1844, Macon Bolling Allen became the first black lawyer when he was admitted to Maine's bar following a period of private study (Hargrove 2010, 752). The first known black law school applicant, John Mercer Langston, was denied regular admission to a private law school in New York because the owner feared upsetting John C. Calhoun, who had promised to send students from South Carolina to the school (Langston 1894, 107). Langston was offered admission, however, if he would consent to one of two conditions. First, Langston could "consent to pass as a Frenchman or a Spaniard hailing from the West India Islands, Central or South America" (107–108). Alternatively, Langston could "edge" his way into the school by satisfying the following requirements: "Come into the recitation room; take your seat off and apart from the class; ask no questions; behave yourself quietly; and if after a time no one says anything against, but all seem well inclined toward you, you may move up nearer the class;

and so continue to do till you are taken and considered in due time as in full and regular membership" (108). Langston refused to meet either condition, but was ultimately admitted to the Ohio bar in 1854 after a period of private study (125).[17]

A few years after the Civil War ended, George Lewis Ruffin became the first black person to receive a degree from an American law school when he graduated from Harvard in 1869 (J. C. Smith 1995, 214). Following Ruffin's landmark achievement, law schools around the country slowly and sporadically began admitting black students (see J. C. Smith 1993, 33–65). This process of diversifying the legal profession continued into the twentieth century, but segregation's pervasive institutionalization served as a substantial roadblock. As one scholar notes, "Racial prejudice, combined with a continuing lack of educational and economic resources, served to curtail seriously the number of blacks who aspired to join the legal profession and limited greatly the range of success and accomplishment for those who somehow overcame these multiple handicaps to law practice" (D. Bell 1970, 541).

Two U.S. Supreme Court cases from the twentieth century offer a glimpse into what legal education was like for black students during segregation while also highlighting *Plessy*'s gradual demise. In *Missouri ex rel. Gaines v. Canada* (1938), the Court began chipping away at *Plessy*'s "separate but equal" foundation by invalidating Missouri's policy offering to pay a black student's way to an out-of-state law school rather than offer admission to the in-state flagship school under the Fourteenth Amendment's Equal Protection Clause. The Court indicated that Missouri could either admit the petitioner or provide a separate law school for black students.[18] In *Sweatt v. Painter* (1950), the Court held that a separate law school established for black students in Texas was not "equal" to the University of Texas's Law School on dimensions such as the "number of the faculty, variety of courses and opportunity for specialization, size of the student body, scope of the library, availability of law review . . . reputation of the faculty, experience of the administration, position and influence of the alumni, standing in the community, traditions and prestige" (633–634).[19]

The U.S. Supreme Court's landmark decision in *Brown v. Board of Education* (1954, 495) declared that "separate educational facilities are inherently unequal," overturning *Plessy* after more than half a century. Notwithstanding *Brown*'s political and legal importance, it was but one part of a broader push for civil rights that also required executive and legislative action (see, e.g., B. Friedman 2009, 237–279; Klarman 2004; G. Rosenberg 2008, 39–169). In 1957, President Dwight Eisenhower signaled executive support for implementation of the Court's ruling when he ordered the military to assist with integration efforts in Little Rock, Arkansas, where the recalcitrant Governor Orval Faubus and local school board were obstructing integration. Moreover, congressional passage of the Civil Rights Act of 1964 and Voting Rights Act of 1965 were essential to furthering integration and reducing barriers to racial equality.

That the federal judiciary started moving toward racial diversification during this period is, of course, not a coincidence. William Henry Hastie became the first black federal judge to sit on an Article III court after President Truman nominated him to the U.S. Court of Appeals for the Third Circuit in 1949 (Rusch 1978, 803).[20] In 1961, James Parsons became the first black district court judge after being appointed by President John F. Kennedy to serve on the U.S. District Court for the Northern District of Illinois (Watson 1987, 267). After a long career as a leading civil rights attorney and shorter stints as the second black federal circuit court judge and first black U.S. solicitor general, Thurgood Marshall became the first black U.S. Supreme Court justice in 1967 after being nominated by President Lyndon Johnson (J. Williams 1998). In 1991, Clarence Thomas replaced Justice Marshall, becoming the Court's second black justice.

The first black state supreme court justice was seated in the postbellum era, although the second would not be seated until the modern civil rights movement was well under way. Named to the South Carolina Supreme Court by the state legislature in 1870, Jonathan Jasper Wright became the first black justice to sit on a state's highest appellate court. Before his appointment to the South Carolina Supreme Court, Wright was the first black person admitted to the Pennsylvania bar and one of the first three simultaneously admitted in South Carolina; he also enjoyed a distinguished political career as state senator and vice president of the 1868 South Carolina Constitutional Convention (Woody 1933). More than ninety years after Wright's appointment,

Otis Smith became the second black state supreme court justice with his appointment to Michigan's highest bench in 1961. After an eight-year span with no other state seating their first black supreme court justice, additional state high courts were increasingly, albeit slowly, diversified beginning in 1969 (see Goelzhauser 2011). Nineteen states, however, had yet to seat their first black supreme court justice through 2014.[21]

Hispanic and Asian American Judges

In recent years, scholars and others have become increasingly interested in racial integration of the judiciary. In particular, there is a growing body of research on Hispanic (e.g., Echaveste 2002; Olmstead 2009; Sotomayor 2002) and Asian American (e.g., Chew and Kelley-Chew 2010; Hsu 2006; Heilman 2008) judges. Furthermore, it is now common for the press to include the number of Hispanic and Asian American judges in their reports about state judicial diversity (e.g., Hancock 2015; Katz 2013; Roig-Franzia 2002). Reynaldo Garza became the first Hispanic federal judge following his nomination to the U.S. District Court for the Southern District of Texas in 1961 by President Kennedy (see Fisch 1996), and Sonia Sotomayor became the first Hispanic justice to serve on the U.S. Supreme Court following her nomination by President Obama 2009. Herbert Choy became the first Asian American federal judge following his nomination to the U.S. Court of Appeals for the Ninth Circuit in 1971 by President Nixon (Chew and Kelley-Chew 2010, 181–182). Unfortunately, little comprehensive information is available about Hispanic and Asian American state judges. Eugene Lujan, elected to the New Mexico Supreme Court in 1945, was the first Hispanic state supreme court justice I was able to identify (Padilla 1974; New Mexico Supreme Court 2010). And Masiji Marumoto, appointed to the Hawaii Supreme Court in 1959, was the first Asian American state supreme court justice I was able to identify.[22]

Selection Systems and Diversity

The previous section demonstrates that early struggles toward judicial diversification focused on overcoming formal and informal barriers to legal education and equal access to professional opportunities. As a result, the question of which selection systems were more conducive to seating political minorities received little attention. There is no indication in the historical record that concern with judicial diversity played a prominent role in the early debates over merit selection. One of the first known connections between merit selection and diversity occurred in Birmingham, Alabama. When the city adopted merit selection for its local judges in 1950, a desire to insulate the white establishment from increasing black electoral power might have been an important motivation (Shugerman 2012, 218–223). In many states, the League of Women Voters, a civic organization created just before the Nineteenth Amendment's ratification to facilitate women's involvement in political affairs, played an important role in the push for merit selection (see, e.g., R. Clark 2006, 4). However, minimizing the extent to which judges were beholden to political pressures in order to make the judiciary more representative and transparent—not increasing the number of women judges—seems to have been the group's primary goal at the time (see, e.g., Felice and Kilwein 1992, 195).

The connection between merit selection and judicial diversity gained considerable traction with President Carter's efforts to diversify the federal judiciary after taking office in 1977.[23] As noted in Chapter 4, President Carter instituted merit-based selection commissions to identify and screen candidates for circuit court judgeships; he also encouraged senators to create merit-based selection commissions to identify and screen candidates for district court judgeships. Scholars often attribute the "groundbreaking" (M. Clark 2011, 1132) diversification of the federal judiciary under President Carter in substantial part to these merit commissions (e.g., Tobias 1993, 1259–1261). By "significantly expand[ing] the number and types of people participating in the process of federal judicial selection" (Martin 1987, 140), more political minorities were considered and nominated for judicial vacancies under Carter than in previous years. Accordingly, "the key to Carter's success . . . was not to ignore merit, but to rely upon it" with the view that "the 'old boys' network' could not be trusted to identify all the able candidates" (Ginsburg and Brill 1995, 288).

The argument that Carter's merit commissions would benefit political minorities as a result of deemphasizing the role political

connections played in obtaining judgeships naturally coincided with
the general argument in favor of merit selection being advanced at
the state level (see, e.g., Crompton 2002, 766). As a result, it is now
commonplace for merit selection's proponents to contend that adopting merit selection will increase diversity on state courts by removing
the long-standing barriers that political minorities face in attempting
to secure judgeships through selection processes that rely on unilateral
nomination or popular election (see, e.g., Douglass 1977, 685; Goldstein 2007, 370; Kruse 2001, 75). As one scholar put it, "there is no
question but that the merit selection system affords greater opportunities for women and minorities to find their way to the bench" (Krivosha
1987, 19). But critics often publicly wonder whether merit selection
might actually impede judicial diversification (see, e.g., Krajelis 2012;
"Keep Courts on Track" 1996; Talbott 1987).

The empirical literature on the relationship between judicial selection systems and diversity is rich and varied. Although the overall results are mixed, on balance the literature suggests that selection
systems play little role in state supreme court diversification.[24] Some
of these studies rely on descriptive statistics for comparison. Looking at
the pool of state supreme court justices serving in 1999, one study concludes that "white men appear to fare best under [merit selection]" on
the basis of evidence that "42.7% of white male justices were selected
in states with merit plans, compared to 31.8% of black males, [and]
33.3% of white females, and black females" (Martin and Pyle 2002,
48). The study, however, offers no indication of whether these differences are statistically significant. Analyzing data on all state appellate
judges serving in 1985 and 1999, Mark Hurwitz and Drew Lanier
(2001) found that more nonwhite males had been seated through non-
merit selection systems in 1985, but the difference in 1999 was not
statistically distinguishable from zero. A follow-up study using data
on all sitting state appellate court judges in 2005 found that "diversity
is not associated with selection system in the vast majority of cases"
(Hurwitz and Lanier 2008, 53). Suggesting that "the majority of [ex-
isting] studies are based on the court's formal method of selection and
do not take into account the method by which judges were actually
selected," an analysis of state supreme court justices serving in 2008
demonstrates that a majority of the justices who were racial minorities,

and a plurality of female justices, obtained their seats through merit selection (Reddick, Nelson, and Caufield 2009).

In addition to these descriptive comparisons, several multivariate analyses have been undertaken. One early empirical study found no relationship between merit selection and the percentage of female or minority state judges in 1985 (Alozie 1990). Analyzing data from 1985 and 1999, Hurwitz and Lanier (2003) found no relationship between selection system and the number of women serving on state appellate courts.[25] Another study found little relationship between selection method and the length of time that passed until a state seated its first female and black supreme court justice (Goelzhauser 2011). Additional studies analyze the relationship between selection system and the seating of female or nonwhite judges (but not both). One study, for example, found no relationship between merit selection and the percentage of female supreme court justices or whether a female supreme court justice served in 1993 (Alozie 1996). Analyzing data from 2003, Margaret Williams (2007) found that merit selection was not associated with the number of female state trial court judges but was negatively associated with the number of female appellate court judges. Using a database of all judges seated on state supreme courts from 1980 through 1997, Kathleen Bratton and Rorie Spill (2002) find that women were more likely to be appointed to the bench than seated through election, but they do not distinguish between unilateral appointment and merit selection.

Although fewer studies have focused exclusively on the relationship between selection system and the seating of black judges, the results on this question are similarly mixed. Using a sample of nearly four thousand trial court judges across thirty-six states, Barbara Luck Graham (1990) found that black judges were generally no more likely to be seated under merit selection than under legislative appointment; states that used merit selection for interim appointments, however, were more likely to seat black judges for interim appointments compared to legislative appointment. Using a one-year sample across forty-seven states, Nicholas Alozie (1988) found no relationship between selection system and the number of black judges.

Although each of the existing empirical studies offers important contributions for our understanding of the connection between selection systems and diversity, several limitations hinder our ability to draw conclusions about whether merit selection has made any difference for placing political minorities on state supreme courts. As an initial matter, not all studies of the connection between selection system and diversification isolate the effect of merit selection. Moreover, when the effect of merit selection is isolated there is often no accounting for the different ways a single state's judges can be seated. This accounting is particularly important for evaluating the consequences of merit selection given that some states use merit selection for interim seatings but not otherwise. Last, most empirical studies use data from one or two years, which limits our ability to draw inferences about merit selection's long-term performance.

Empirical Analysis

To examine whether any judicial selection system is more likely than another to produce judges who are women or racial minorities, I use the database of state supreme court justices seated from 1960 through 2014 described in Chapter 3 and Appendix A. Using automated content analysis to code gender on the basis of the gender breakdown of first names in census data, Adam Bonica and Michael Woodruff's (2015) list of state supreme court justices serving between 1990 and 2012 incorrectly classifies some justices' gender. I corrected information for incorrectly classified justices and updated and backdated the information using biographical records for other justices in the database. Given that systematic information about state supreme court justices' race is not available, I collected this information through biographical searches.[26]

Dependent Variables

There are four dependent variables in the ensuing analysis. In the female justices model, the dependent variable is an indicator scored one if a female justice filled a given opening and zero otherwise. In the black justices model, the dependent variable is an indicator scored one if a black justice filled a given opening and zero otherwise. In the nonwhite justices model, the dependent variable is an indicator scored

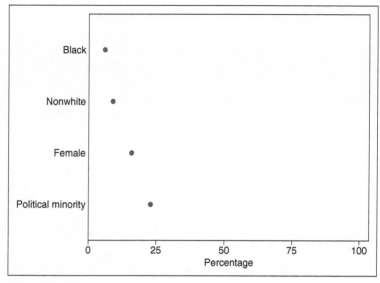

Figure 5.1 Summary statistics: diversity

one if a black, Hispanic, or Asian American justice filled a given open-ing and zero otherwise.[27] In the political minorities model (cf. Hurwitz and Lanier 2003), the dependent variable is an indicator scored one if a female, black, Hispanic, or Asian American justice filled a given opening and zero otherwise. Figure 5.1 plots summary information for each dependent variable. From 1960 through 2014, 16 percent of state supreme court seatings were filled by females, 6 percent by blacks, 2 percent by Hispanics, and 1 percent by Asian Americans. Overall, 23 percent of seatings during the sample period were filled by political minorities.[28]

Independent Variables

There are two key explanatory variables. First, the appointment vari-able is scored one for justices who were seated by elite appointment and zero otherwise. Second, the election variable is scored one for justices who were seated through partisan or nonpartisan election and zero otherwise. Merit selection is the excluded baseline. Figure 5.2 plots

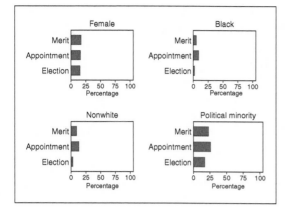

Figure 5.2
Summary statistics by selection system: gender and racial diversity

summary statistics for each dependent variable across the three major selection systems. In addition to the key explanatory variables, several control variables, described in greater detail in Chapter 3, are included: a measure of court professionalism, court size, term years, mandatory retirement, and state liberalism. While previous analyses included a control for the supply of lawyers in a state, the models employed here include more specific measures to capture the size of each eligibility pool. The female justices model includes the natural log of the number of female lawyers in a state; the black justices model that of black lawyers; the nonwhite justices model that of nonwhite lawyers; and the political minority justices model that of female and nonwhite lawyers.[29] As with previous analyses, the models also include region fixed effects and a cubic polynomial approximation to account for temporal dynamics.

Analysis and Results

Given that each dependent variable is binary, the models are fit with logistic regression. Standard errors are clustered by state to account for nonindependence within states. For interested readers, Table B5 in Appendix B presents the complete multivariate results for each model. Although the estimated coefficients and standard errors in these tables provide information about statistical significance, they do not convey readily interpretable information about substantive impact. To provide

easy-to-interpret information about substantive differences across selection systems, Table 5.1 presents changes in predicted probabilities
associated with the various diversity-related outcomes moving from
the first listed selection institution to the second.[30] Table 5.1 also includes 95 percent confidence intervals around the predicted change
in probability, indicating whether the difference is statistically distinguishable from zero at that threshold.

Although no selection system is consistently more likely than others to seat women and racial minorities as state supreme court justices,
there are important differences across systems. The probability of seating a female justice increases from 8 percent (95 percent confidence
interval of 5 percent, 10 percent) under merit selection to 13 percent
(10 percent, 16 percent) under appointment, a change of 5 percent
(2 percent, 8 percent). The difference in probability between seating a
female justice under merit selection or election is not statistically distinguishable from zero, and neither is that of seating a female justice
under appointment or election.

Differences in the probability of seating black and nonwhite justices more generally under merit selection and appointment are not
statistically distinguishable from zero. However, the probability of
seating black and nonwhite justices is lower on average under election
than either merit selection or appointment. The probability of seating

TABLE 5.1 CHANGE IN QUANTITIES OF INTEREST: DIVERSITY

	Merit vs. appointment	Merit vs. election	Appointment vs. election
Female	5%*	2%	–4%
	(2%, 8%)	(–2%, 5%)	(–7%, 1%)
Black	1%	–3%*	–4%*
	(–1%, 3%)	(–5%, –1%)	(–7%, –2%)
Nonwhite	3%	–5%*	–8%*
	(–2%, 8%)	(–9%, –1%)	(–12%, –4%)
Political minority	11%*	–4%	–15%*
	(4%, 18%)	(–9%, 1%)	(–20%, –10%)

Note: Numbers outside parentheses are changes in predicted probabilities moving from the first selection system to the second. Parentheses contain 95 percent confidence intervals. Results from the full
models that generated these results are presented in Table B5 in Appendix B.
*p < 0.05 (two-tailed).

a black justice decreases from 4 percent (2 percent, 6 percent) under merit selection to 1 percent (<1 percent, >1 percent) under election, a change of –3 percent (–5 percent, –1 percent). Similarly, the probability of seating a black justice decreases from 5 percent (2 percent, 7 percent) under appointment to 1 percent (<1 percent, >1 percent) under election, a change of –4 percent (–7 percent, –2 percent). The probability of seating any nonwhite state supreme court justice decreases from 7 percent (3 percent, 11 percent) under merit selection to 2 percent (<1 percent, 3 percent) under election, a change of –5 percent (–9 percent, –1 percent). Furthermore, the probability of seating any nonwhite justice decreases from 10 percent (5 percent, 14 percent) under appointment to 2 percent (1 percent, 3 percent) under election, a change of –8 percent (–12 percent, –4 percent). This means that merit selection and appointment systems yield about two and three more nonwhite justices, respectively, for every thirty seatings on average compared to election.

Appointment systems are more likely on average to seat political minorities, which is the category that combines female, black, Hispanic, and Asian American justices. Moving from merit selection to appointment is associated with an increase in the probability of seating a political minority from 15 percent (11 percent, 20 percent) to 26 percent (19 percent, 33 percent), a change of 11 percent (4 percent, 18 percent). Moving from appointment to election, meanwhile, is associated with a decrease in the probability of seating a political minority from 26 percent (19 percent, 33 percent) to 11 percent (7 percent, 15 percent), a change of –15 percent (–20 percent, –10 percent). The difference in probability between seating a political minority under merit selection and election is not statistically distinguishable from zero.[31]

Turning to the control variables, three results are worth noting. In the black justices model, an increase in the natural log of black lawyers in a state from one standard deviation below its mean to one standard deviation above is associated with an increase in the probability of seating a black justice from 3 percent (1 percent, 5 percent) to 10 percent (5 percent, 14 percent), a change of 7 percent (3 percent, 12 percent). In the nonwhite justices model, an increase in the natural log of nonwhite lawyers in a state from one standard deviation below its mean to one standard deviation above is associated with an increase in the probability of seating a nonwhite justice from 3 percent (1 percent, 6 percent) to 17 percent (8 percent, 26 percent), a change of 14 percent (5 percent, 23 percent). Last, an increase in state liberalism from one standard deviation below its mean to one standard deviation above is associated with an increase in the probability of seating a political minority from 21 percent (15 percent, 26 percent) to 33 percent (23 percent, 43 percent), a change of 12 percent (4 percent, 21 percent).

Conclusion

Unlike qualifications, diversity has not historically played an important role in debates over judicial selection. Indeed, women and racial minorities struggled just to gain access to the legal profession as many of the early judicial selection debates unfolded. As formal and informal barriers began to crack, women and racial minorities increasingly obtained access to the legal profession albeit on unequal footing. The process of diversifying state supreme courts proceeded slowly and is still taking place, mirroring efforts to diversify the federal judiciary. President Carter's experimentation with merit panels at the federal level might have influenced perspectives on the connection between state judicial selection institutions and diversification, with merit selection's proponents increasingly contending that their favored system led to more opportunities for women and racial minorities by deemphasizing the role that political connections have historically played in judicial selection decisions. Merit selection's critics, meanwhile, suggest that it makes no difference at best and may in fact be worse for women and racial minorities. Notwithstanding an extensive literature on the connection between judicial selection institutions and judicial diversity, convincing empirical answers have remained elusive.

The results presented in this chapter suggest that selection systems matter for the diversification of state supreme courts but not necessarily in a consistent way. No selection system produces more or less diverse state supreme court justices across categories. Nonetheless, there is some evidence of a relationship between selection institutions and diversification. Merit selection is less likely than appointment on average to produce justices who are females or political minorities, and more likely than election to produce justices who are black or nonwhite more generally. In addition, elections are less likely than appointment systems on average to produce justices who are black, nonwhite, or political minorities. Overall, the empirical results suggest that the relationship between selection institutions and judicial diversity is more nuanced than the rhetoric that often drives this debate would suggest.

Analysis of the relationship between judicial selection systems and diversity should, of course, continue. As discussed earlier, racial groups such as Hispanics and Asian Americans are only just beginning to be considered more readily for state supreme court vacancies. In 2003, Rives Kistler became the first openly LGBTQ person to serve on a state supreme court when he was appointed to Oregon's bench (Haider-Markel 2010, 106). And the study of intersectionality on state supreme courts remains in its infancy. Future studies will continue to advance our understanding of these issues and the consequences that selection systems have for state court diversification. With respect to merit selection in particular, future work would benefit from exploring issues such as whether commission-specific rules or composition is associated with changes in diversification.

6 | Conclusion

Merit selection is the latest innovation during a long period of state-led institutional experimentation with respect to judicial selection. Notwithstanding the long historical debate over these selection institutions, solid empirical foundations regarding their consequences have been slow to develop. Using new data on state supreme court seatings from 1960 through 2014, the results presented here lend considerable nuance and insight to the ongoing policy discussion over merit selection. Moreover, contrasting merit selection with its popular alternatives informs our broader understanding of comparative institutional performance with respect to state judicial selection. Although scholars, policy makers, and other stakeholders may be in the midst of an "endless judicial selection debate" (Geyh 2008), moving the discussion forward requires unraveling the empirical consequences of institutional reform. I advance this goal here by presenting the most extensive analysis to date on the relationship between judicial selection institutions and the characteristics of individuals chosen to serve on state supreme courts. The results suggest that no judicial selection system enjoys a systematic advantage over the others.

Summary of Findings

Before moving to the empirical analyses that make up the book's nucleus, Chapter 2 traces merit selection's origins to locate the contemporary policy debate in historical context. Although the process by which federal judges are selected has remained relatively stable since the U.S. Constitution's ratification in 1789, states have experimented with a variety of institutional frameworks for selecting judges since the first Revolutionary-era state constitutions were adopted. While the first state constitutions implemented judicial appointment systems modeled after English and colonial practice, states quickly began experimenting with electing judges. Following a period of gradual institutional development and state-specific political shocks that resulted in dissatisfaction with dominant selection systems, merit selection's first iterations appeared early in the twentieth century, before Missouri first adopted it for supreme court justices in 1940. It is commonly noted that all methods of selecting judges are political, and Chapter 3's tales of institutional experimentation support this proposition while also placing contemporary discussions in historical context.

Chapter 3 analyzes the connection between judicial selection institutions and the professional experience amassed by individuals selected to serve on state supreme courts. Although this was one of the first questions raised by scholars studying the consequences of judicial selection institutions, the literature has developed largely atheoretically, aside from attempts to answer questions about the relationship between merit selection and the political connectedness of chosen judges. Nonetheless, burgeoning literatures on the value of experiential diversity for collegial courts and the relationship between professional experience and judicial behavior encourage new inquiries into whether certain selection systems sort on particular types of professional experience. Analyzing new employment categories that may have important theoretical implications for judicial behavior, the results presented in Chapter 3 reveal no systematic differences across selection systems. One important finding, however, was that merit systems are less likely than appointment or election on average to produce justices with major political office experience. This result can be leveraged in support of or against merit selection depending on whether one emphasizes it as a proxy for the importance of political connections or as evidence that a pool of prospective justices many believe to be underrepresented in the judiciary are less likely to be chosen.

Merit selection's core promise to produce better-qualified judges is evaluated in Chapter 4. The chapter demonstrates that the centuries-old debate over how to design judicial selection institutions has emphasized qualifications at every turn, with advocates of every selection system claiming that their favored institution would produce a better-qualified judiciary. This background helps place the contemporary emphasis on qualifications in the debate over merit selection in historical context. Notwithstanding the long-running and contentious debates, the empirical results suggest that selection systems yield similarly qualified state supreme court justices. Indeed, none of the differences across selection systems with respect to various measures of judicial experience are statistically distinguishable from zero. Election underperforms merit selection and appointment on certain measures of educational quality and performance, but not uniformly. And merit selection and elite appointment perform similarly across every measure of judicial qualifications examined.

While the debate over merit selection, and judicial selection institutions more broadly, has long emphasized qualifications, recent decades have seen increasing attention being paid to diversity. Early debates over how to design state judicial selection institutions occurred as women and racial minorities struggled to overcome formal and informal barriers restricting access to the legal profession. Following the increased political attention to judicial diversity brought about during President Carter's tenure, debate grew over which selection system best fostered diversification. Currently, it is common for merit selection's proponents to argue that their favored system enhances judicial diversity, while critics suggest otherwise. The empirical results presented in Chapter 5 assess comparative institutional performance with respect to producing diverse state supreme court justices. Merit selection is less likely than appointment on average to yield justices who are female or political minorities broadly defined. However, merit selection is more likely than election to yield justices who are black or nonwhite.

Appointment systems are more likely than election to yield justices who are black, nonwhite, or political minorities broadly defined.

Normative Implications

What do these results mean for the normative debate over how to design judicial selection institutions? Fleshing out the normative implications of quantitative research is particularly important when, as is the case here, empirical results bear directly on arguments being made in policy circles with respect to institutional reform (Bartels and Bonneau 2015). As an initial matter, taken together the results presented here counsel skepticism regarding any claim that one selection system enjoys systematic empirical advantages over others with respect to producing state supreme court justices with characteristics having to do with professional experience, qualifications, and diversity. Although no single study is definitive, the results presented here are largely consistent with previous research—using different methods and data— finding that judicial selection systems tend to exhibit more similarity than differences when it comes to the characteristics of individuals selected to serve on state supreme courts.

I emphasize, however, that one judicial selection system failing to outperform the others does not mean that selection institutions do not matter. This leads to the second important normative implication, which is that more precision should be used when referring to the consequences of institutional design choices concerning judicial selection. Although saying that merit selection outperforms election when it comes to diversifying state supreme courts appears to be somewhat misleading, the results presented in Chapter 5, for example, do suggest that openings filled by merit selection are more likely on average to yield black or nonwhite justices than under election, while there is no meaningful observable difference with respect to women. And while saying that merit selection outperforms election appears to be somewhat misleading given the similarity between the two across numerous dimensions, the results presented in Chapter 4 do suggest that openings filled by merit selection are more likely on average to yield justices who attended an elite law school and performed well academically.

The rub is determining how to weight the existing empirical evidence. One approach would be to afford equal weight to each outcome assessed here, aggregate the results from pairwise comparisons of selection institutions, and declare a round-robin winner. Of course, few will find this approach appealing. But the counterfactual highlights that the alternative, aside from declaring all the empirical results useless, is to make difficult decisions about the relative weight to afford various outcomes: Which professional backgrounds should be most valued? How much previous judicial experience should prospective state supreme court justices have? Is raw intelligence important? To what extent should concern about judicial diversity prevail over other objectives? And what types of diversity are most important? Surely reasonable people can disagree about the answers to these questions. In doing so, however, it is important for stakeholders to be transparent about their preference orderings with respect to what they want a judicial selection system to accomplish (cf. Tarr 2007, 295–297). After considering the results presented here, for example, two readers may come away with very different positions on the most efficacious selection institution if one thinks that prior judicial experience is the most important characteristic to consider while the other is most interested in promoting racial diversity.

Comprehensively considering the normative question also requires incorporating a wealth of additional information. One plausible approach to deciding how to weight the empirical results presented here is to determine whether, for example, professional background influences judicial behavior, whether better-qualified judges write better opinions, and whether judicial diversity influences public perceptions of institutional legitimacy. If variation in certain ex ante qualifications has no observable impact on ex post outcomes concerning topics such as judicial behavior and public opinion, it may be difficult to make a strong case for adopting selection institutions that sort on those ex ante qualifications. Instead, stakeholders may focus on characteristics that translate into observable outcomes that people care about. As scholars continue to advance our understanding of these ancillary questions, their efforts inform the ever-developing judicial selection debate. And in this way the debate over judicial selection institutions is inextricably linked to other important inquiries involving law and politics.

Aggregating existing knowledge about the consequences of judicial selection institutions is also essential for fully engaging the normative debate. Every new piece of evidence about the consequences of judicial selection institutions "adds to extant findings that collectively can be used to assess the benefits and pitfalls of any selection scheme" (Melinda Gann Hall 2015, xvi). Although the outcomes assessed in this book are fundamental considerations in the overarching judicial selection debate, they certainly do not exhaust the list of potentially important characteristics to consider when evaluating the consequences of various institutional design choices. Moreover, there is more to evaluating judicial selection institutions than understanding how they sort on particular characteristics. Other important considerations, which have been addressed extensively in the literature, include understanding how judicial selection institutions are related to judicial behavior, proclivities toward professional misconduct, and public perceptions of institutional legitimacy.

The empirical results presented here and elsewhere must also be considered in conjunction with arguments for and against particular judicial selection institutions grounded in democratic theory. Perhaps the most common argument against merit selection, although it applies to other appointive systems as well, is that voters should determine who holds judicial office (e.g., Olszewski 2004; Schneider 2010; Uehlein and Wilderman 2002). One scholar, for example, claims that "merit selection is inherently perilous to a well-functioning democracy and is fundamentally illegitimate because it permits groups of selected elites, not the People, to choose our policymakers, i.e., judges" (Bopp 2013, 87). Although this position can be debated as a matter of democratic theory (see, e.g., Caufield 2011; Russell 2008), those who consider the basic point dispositive are unlikely to be swayed from supporting elections regardless of updated information about the consequences of different selection institutions. But those for whom democratic values are but one consideration among many in choosing a favored judicial selection system must determine how to weight it relative to other available information about institutional performance.

Future Research

There are several important avenues for future research concerning judicial selection and merit selection in particular.[1] First, our understanding of comparative institutional performance with respect to state judicial selection is likely to improve as scholars continue to devise new ways to address important measurement issues. Lack of additional progress on this front is attributable in part to the overuse of ill-defined concepts in the popular debate over judicial selection. Arguments about whether political connections are more or less important under merit selection, for example, cannot be meaningfully evaluated without stakeholders clarifying what they mean when they invoke the phrase. This applies to other important concepts as well, including judicial qualifications and temperament. As a result, many competing claims involving core features of the judicial selection debate are made without opportunity for meaningful refutation. Additional clarity on these fronts will undoubtedly help scholars develop new ways to measure important concepts such as judicial qualifications and political connections that can be used to further our understanding of the consequences of institutional design choices concerning judicial selection.

One important, and largely unanswered, question related to merit selection is whether these systems ineffectually decrease the candidate pool. In a traditional appointment system, the governor is free to select anyone who satisfies the state's minimum judicial service qualifications. Given that these minimum qualifications are often not particularly limiting, the governor enjoys a good deal of discretion in searching out highly qualified people who might not otherwise consider applying for a vacancy under merit selection.[2] Highly qualified people might not apply for judicial vacancies for several reasons, including reluctance to accept a lower salary, unease at entering the public spotlight, or expected professional reputation costs if rejected. Of course, the political history surrounding judicial appointments demonstrates that having a large pool of qualified candidates does not ensure the selection of highly qualified but reluctant prospective judges. Nonetheless, it is important to develop a better sense of how the merit selection process shapes the pool of candidates. This could be particularly important if members of historically underrepresented groups in the judiciary such as women and racial minorities tend to shy away from submitting applications because of perceptions about the importance of factors such as political connections in the selection process.

As scholars develop a better sense of the candidate pools that merit selection systems generate, they can carefully consider what influences commission decisions to forward certain individuals over others to the appointment stage. The empirical literature on merit selection thus far has largely focused on the characteristics of those ultimately picked to serve on state supreme courts. But this is merely the last decision in the merit selection process. Whether merit selection commissions do a good job sorting on characteristics such as qualifications at the first stage is still unknown. If a commission ultimately fails to forward a short list of qualified candidates, even a hypothetical apolitical governor could do little in most instances other than satisfice by selecting the best person from the list. Unfortunately, it is difficult to evaluate a commission's performance in this regard because application information is often not made publicly available. Relatedly, little is known about gubernatorial choice from the list of candidates supplied by the commission. Ideally, commissions would make information on all applicants, and the list of forwarded names, publicly available. This would allow scholars to take the two-stage nature of merit selection seriously. Rectifying these data limitations would improve our understanding of how merit selection operates.

Another comparatively underexplored question is whether the design of merit selection commissions influences outcomes that people care about. In general, scholars and policy makers tend to treat merit selection commissions as institutionally homogeneous. The reality, however, is that there is considerable variation in commission structure and procedure across states (see, e.g., Caufield 2007; Fitzpatrick 2009). Differences exist, for example, over the ability of stakeholders such as the governor, legislature, and state bar association to select commissioners. States also differ over the extent to which lawyers and nonlawyers are included in commissions. Some states have formal rules ensuring a bipartisan commission while others do not. And procedures concerning commission governance also vary, with different rules regarding questions such as whether the commission plays an active role in seeking out qualified applicants. Determining whether certain institutional design choices are more conducive to securing favorable outcomes is an important next step in the quest to evaluate merit selection's institutional performance.

Issues involving the commissioners are related to broader questions concerning institutional design. Who serves on these commissions? What types of commissioners are various stakeholders likely to appoint? The answers to these questions could have important implications for merit selection's performance. One of the commonly noted features of merit selection is that commissions typically include lawyers and nonlawyers. The inclusion of nonlawyers is thought to bring an element of objectivity, political detachment, and democratic representation to the merit selection process. But the extent to which these objectives are achieved may depend on which nonlawyers are selected. One could imagine a difference, for example, between designating a randomly selected nonlawyer citizen (similar to a jury) versus a politically active nonlawyer with close ties to the governor. The point is not that either of these hypothetical individuals would necessarily be good or bad commission members. Rather, the question is whether people with varying incentives, backgrounds, and capabilities approach the selection process in different ways. The first step toward answering these questions is to learn more about the commissioners.

Further developing our understanding of merit selection's institutional performance also necessitates its consideration in the context of lower court judicial appointments. Political scientists have made important contributions to the study of judicial selection and retention issues concerning trial (e.g., Dubois 1984; Huber and Gordon 2004) and intermediate appellate (e.g., Frederick and Streb 2008; Streb, Frederick, and LaFrance 2009) courts. Nonetheless, comparatively little has been written about merit selection for lower court judges. State supreme court vacancies can be major political events that attract acute interest from various stakeholders—a stark contrast from the relative invisibility of many lower court appointments. It could be that merit selection performs well with respect to lower court appointments but tends to break down under the glaring light and high stakes that can accompany supreme court vacancies.

Last Words

In the end, determining which judicial selection system is "best" may be futile, but its study informs our understanding of judicial politics and institutional performance while simultaneously contributing to an important ongoing policy debate. As we continue this discussion, stakeholders need to address the first-principles question of what we want judicial selection institutions to accomplish. To the extent that people disagree about its answer, definitive statements about which system is best are likely to prove illusory. In the interim, the mosaic of research on state courts depicts an impressive collection of insights into the comparative institutional performance of judicial selection systems. This book contributes to this mosaic by analyzing the relationship between judicial selection systems and the characteristics of those chosen to be state supreme court justices. The results suggest that there are important differences even if no selection system consistently outperforms the others. With merit selection in particular, the evidence suggests that it sometimes outperforms, sometimes underperforms, and mostly performs similarly to other systems depending on the outcome of interest. These results are consistent with the debate's overarching complexity.

Appendix A: Data Collection

To assemble a list of state supreme court justices seated from 1960 through 2014, I began with the list of justices compiled by Adam Bonica and Michael Woodruff (2015). Their list included most of the justices who served at some point from 1990 through 2012. Next, I extended this list through the end of 2014 and backdated it to 1960 using lists provided by state supreme courts, historical societies, various volumes of the Council of State Governments' *Book of the States*, and other sources. The resulting list includes, to the best of my knowledge, every state supreme court justice seated from 1960 through 2014. The list does not include justices who served temporarily, for example, pending an ill justice returning or a vacancy being formally filled. Temporary appointments are different from interim appointments, however, which are included. The seating decision is the event that led to the individual becoming a justice rather than the actual start date. For example, a justice elected to fill a state supreme court vacancy in November 2012 but beginning service in January 2013 is treated as a 2012 seating.

After compiling the list, I used a variety of sources to collect background information about those individuals. For most of the justices who had recently served or are still serving, reasonably complete biographical statements are available online through state supreme court websites or news articles. Other sources include archived newspaper articles, law review articles, bar journals, obituaries, remembrances, law firm web pages, and biographical databases accessed through LexisNexis. For some justices, certain types of information could not be located.

APPENDIX B: TABLES OF RESULTS

Tables B1–B5 display results from the multivariate models discussed in Chapters 3, 4, and 5. Details about the variables and estimation are included in the chapters.

TABLE B1   EXPERIENCE: THE PUBLIC-PRIVATE DISTINCTION

	Public only	Private only	Public and private
Appointment	0.10	−0.46*	0.38*
	(0.23)	(0.15)	(0.13)
Election	0.18	−0.09	0.01
	(0.28)	(0.19)	(0.15)
Court professionalism	−0.18	0.87	−0.63
	(0.73)	(0.50)	(0.45)
Court size	−0.05	0.07	−0.04
	(0.07)	(0.06)	(0.05)
Term years	−0.02	0.01	0.01
	(0.02)	(0.01)	(0.02)
Mandatory retirement	−0.24	−0.15	0.25
	(0.17)	(0.14)	(0.13)
ln(lawyers)	−0.67	0.75*	−0.29
	(0.42)	(0.24)	(0.26)
State liberalism	0.02*	−0.01	−0.01
	(0.01)	(0.01)	(0.01)
Intercept	1.32	−6.33*	2.95
	(2.85)	(1.78)	(1.86)
Observations	1,523	1,523	1,523
Region fixed effects	Yes	Yes	Yes
Cubic polynomial	Yes	Yes	Yes

Note: Standard errors are clustered by state and in parentheses. Merit selection is the excluded baseline.
*$p < 0.05$ (two-tailed).

TABLE B2   EXPERIENCE: PUBLIC SERVICE VARIETIES

	Major office	Office ties	Federal government	Prosecutor	Professor	Legal services
Appointment	0.95*	0.66*	1.13*	0.62	0.30	0.17
	(0.28)	(0.23)	(0.42)	(0.33)	(0.38)	(0.57)
Election	1.14*	0.40	0.53	0.47	−0.66	0.23
	(0.27)	(0.26)	(0.50)	(0.40)	(0.45)	(0.61)
Court profes-sionalism	−0.63	−1.47*	−2.82*	0.31	0.93	−0.40
	(0.81)	(0.63)	(1.44)	(0.84)	(1.16)	(1.35)
Court size	−0.17	−0.07	−0.29*	−0.01	0.17	−0.12
	(0.11)	(0.07)	(0.13)	(0.08)	(0.13)	(0.16)
Term years	−0.03	−0.01	0.03	−0.01	0.05	0.08
	(0.04)	(0.02)	(0.06)	(0.02)	(0.04)	(0.05)
Mandatory retirement	0.48*	0.12	0.63	0.10	−0.14	0.20
	(0.24)	(0.15)	(0.51)	(0.22)	(0.32)	(0.31)
ln(lawyers)	−0.18	−0.29	−1.88	−0.72	−0.57	6.22
	(0.31)	(0.33)	(1.03)	(0.58)	(0.52)	(8.80)
State liberalism	−0.01	0.01	0.01	−0.01	−0.01	0.03*
	(0.01)	(0.01)	(0.02)	(0.01)	(0.01)	(0.01)
Intercept	1.85	0.55	7.47	0.28	−3.02	−63.88
	(2.17)	(2.38)	(7.06)	(3.75)	(3.87)	(73.35)
Observations	1,525	1,523	1,523	1,523	1,523	1,523
Region fixed effects	Yes	Yes	Yes	Yes	Yes	Yes
Cubic polynomial	Yes	Yes	Yes	Yes	Yes	Yes

Note: Standard errors are clustered by state and in parentheses. Merit selection is the excluded baseline.
*$p < 0.05$ (two-tailed).

TABLE B3 QUALIFICATIONS: LAW SCHOOL QUALITY AND PERFORMANCE

	Elite law school	Ordered law school ranking	Locally elite law school	Law review
Appointment	0.23	0.09	0.14	−0.16
	(0.22)	(0.22)	(0.17)	(0.19)
Election	−0.46*	−0.32	−0.01	−0.44*
	(0.23)	(0.20)	(0.20)	(0.21)
Court professionalism	0.78	1.75*	−1.94*	0.89
	(0.60)	(0.84)	(0.58)	(0.69)
Court size	−0.03	0.07	−0.10*	0.03
	(0.09)	(0.08)	(0.05)	(0.07)
Term years	0.01	−0.01	0.01	0.01
	(0.02)	(0.02)	(0.02)	(0.02)
Mandatory retirement	0.23	0.30	0.26	0.02
	(0.19)	(0.23)	(0.16)	(0.16)
ln(lawyers)	−0.13	−0.41	−0.22	0.25
	(0.45)	(0.26)	(0.35)	(0.45)
State liberalism	0.01	0.01	−0.01	−0.01
	(0.01)	(0.01)	(0.01)	(0.01)
Intercept	−0.77	—	2.87	−4.65
	(3.00)	—	(2.24)	(3.29)
Observations	1,533	1,508	1,533	1,085
Region fixed effects	Yes	Yes	Yes	Yes
Cubic polynomial	Yes	Yes	Yes	Yes

Note: Standard errors are clustered by state and in parentheses. Merit selection is the excluded baseline.
*$p < 0.05$ (two-tailed).

TABLE B4   QUALIFICATIONS: JUDICIAL EXPERIENCE

	Any judicial experience	Any judicial years	Appellate experience	Appellate years
Appointment	−0.14 (0.23)	−0.30 (0.20)	0.01 (0.14)	−0.56 (0.38)
Election	−0.10 (0.27)	−0.32 (0.18)	0.03 (0.19)	−0.46 (0.40)
Court professionalism	0.86 (0.81)	0.42 (0.41)	0.28 (0.56)	3.11* (1.21)
Court size	0.04 (0.07)	−0.06 (0.04)	0.10* (0.04)	0.21 (0.21)
Term years	−0.02 (0.02)	−0.01 (0.01)	0.03 (0.02)	0.01 (0.04)
Mandatory retirement	0.16 (0.22)	−0.18 (0.12)	−0.17 (0.18)	0.62 (0.37)
ln(lawyers)	−0.32 (0.32)	0.29 (0.34)	0.10 (0.47)	0.33 (0.86)
State liberalism	−0.01 (0.01)	−0.01 (0.01)	−0.01 (0.01)	0.01 (0.01)
Intercept	3.18 (2.17)	0.18 (3.48)	−2.56 (3.26)	−6.55 (9.67)
Observations	1,537	362	1,069	362
Region fixed effects	Yes	Yes	Yes	Yes
Cubic polynomial	Yes	No	Yes	No

Note: Standard errors are clustered by state and in parentheses. Merit selection is the excluded baseline.
$^*p < 0.05$ (two-tailed).

TABLE B5   DIVERSITY: GENDER AND RACE

	Female justices	Black justices	Nonwhite justices	Political minority justices
Appointment	0.56*	0.25	0.41	0.66*
	(0.15)	(0.24)	(0.38)	(0.22)
Election	0.20	−1.89*	−1.52*	−0.36
	(0.20)	(0.49)	(0.59)	(0.22)
Court professionalism	−0.26	0.42	−0.85	−0.15
	(0.65)	(0.95)	(1.45)	(0.77)
Court size	0.07	0.04	−0.16	0.01
	(0.09)	(0.11)	(0.16)	(0.07)
Term years	0.02	0.02	−0.01	0.01
	(0.01)	(0.03)	(0.03)	(0.01)
Mandatory retirement	0.25	0.43	0.47	0.32
	(0.16)	(0.26)	(0.31)	(0.18)
ln(female lawyers)	0.05			
	(0.09)			
ln(black lawyers)		0.36*		
		(0.12)		
ln(nonwhite lawyers)			0.44*	
			(0.13)	
ln(political minority lawyers)				0.14
				(0.08)
State liberalism	0.01	0.01	0.02	0.02*
	(0.01)	(0.01)	(0.01)	(0.01)
Intercept	−7.52*	−9.88*	−7.92*	−7.13*
	(1.40)	(2.13)	(1.79)	(1.00)
Observations	1,543	1,543	1,543	1,543
Region fixed effects	Yes	Yes	Yes	Yes
Cubic polynomial	Yes	Yes	Yes	Yes

Note: Standard errors are clustered by state and in parentheses. Merit selection is the excluded baseline.
*$p < 0.05$ (two-tailed).

Notes

Chapter 1

1. In some instances, the governor's nomination is then subject to a confirmation process similar to the process for seating federal judges.

2. In 2015, for example, the Kansas House Judiciary Committee approved a proposed constitutional amendment abolishing merit selection for state supreme court justices. See House Committee Report (HCR) 5005 (2015). This was one of several legislative proposals advanced in 2015 designed to abolish merit selection for Kansas Supreme Court justices. See also HCR 5004 (2015), HCR 5006 (2015), and HCR 5012 (2015).

3. In 2015, for example, twenty-one legislators cosponsored a proposed constitutional amendment establishing merit selection for Pennsylvania Supreme Court justices. See House Bill 1336 (2015). In addition, several former governors have voiced their support for merit selection (Murphy 2013). Limited polling data also suggest that many Pennsylvania residents favor a switch to merit selection. In one 2010 poll, for example, 62 percent of respondents favored replacing the state's current system with the merit plan. See Committee for Economic Development 2010.

4. As of September 2014, plans were in place to dissolve the American Judicature Society after more than one hundred years in operation.

5. For reviews of the literature on merit selection, see Glick 1978, Goldschmidt 1994, and Reddick 2002.

6. Of course, this argument also applies to other nonelective systems. In turn, merit selection's proponents often cite the deleterious effects of campaign spending, interest group influence over judicial selection decisions, and campaign speech

(see, e.g., O'Connor 2009; Phillips 2009; Zeidman 2005). However, these arguments are often about the perceived pitfalls of electing judges rather than the benefits of merit selection. Indeed, little in these arguments supports adopting merit selection over another nonelective system, such as unilateral elite appointment. Although arguments such as these may be important for the broader debate over choice of judicial selection institution, I do not address them further here because they do not distinguish between merit and other nonelective systems.

7. In a retention election, voters simply choose whether to keep incumbents in office. Notwithstanding the absence of challengers in retention elections, they are more competitive than commonly assumed (Melinda Gann Hall 2001a). For more on the origins and operation of retention elections, see Tarr 2009.

8. Similarly, retention elections can be combined with any selection method.

9. See Rhode Island Constitution, Article X.

10. See Proposing Amendment to Oregon Constitution Relating to Selection of Judges, House Joint Resolution 15 (2015). Hawaii combines merit selection with commission-based reappointment.

11. Debates over judicial selection and retention are not necessarily distinct. In judicial elections, a single race often involves the choice between retaining an incumbent and seating a challenger.

12. For a sample of articles with a variety of counts, see Choi, Gulati, and Posner 2010; Kang and Shepherd 2011; McLeod 2012; Newman and Isaacs 2004; and Zaccari 2004.

13. See California Constitution, Article VI, Section 16.

14. An exception could arise, for example, if sitting justices were exempted from a new institutional rule.

15. This table was constructed using information provided by the American Judicature Society and other documents regarding judicial selection at the state level. Much of the information on voluntary merit selection plans comes from Lowe 1971 and Vandenberg 1983.

16. The lists of voluntary plans are likely incomplete because of a lack of comprehensive accounting for voluntary plans instituted over time.

17. See Tennessee Constitution, Article VI (amended November 2014).

18. This is not to say that all voluntary merit selection systems are transient. Maryland's voluntary merit selection system, for example, has endured for decades. Although the complexities involving merit selection ensure that some arbitrary choice must be made when making classification decisions, distinguishing between voluntary and nonvoluntary plans seems less arbitrary than any rule that would distinguish between particular voluntary plans, especially in light of the fact that the universe of nonvoluntary plans is known, whereas there is no certainty regarding which states have employed voluntary merit selection plans or when they were employed.

19. Caseload data for state supreme courts over this period come from Hall and Windett 2013. Caseload data for the U.S. Supreme Court over this period come from the Supreme Court Database (Spaeth et al. 2014).

20. There is evidence that state supreme courts strategically shape their dockets (Brace and Hall 2001) and that discretionary docket control affects decision making (Melinda Gann Hall 1985).

21. A state supreme court's decision with respect to a question concerning federal law can be appealed. However, the U.S. Supreme Court will review a state court decision that rests on state and federal grounds only if there is no adequate and independent state ground for the ruling. In practice, the U.S. Supreme Court reviews comparatively few cases appealed from state courts each year. As a result, most state supreme court decisions resolving federal questions are final, at least for the immediate parties.

22. Chief Justice John Roberts of the U.S. Supreme Court famously defended the judges-as-automaton perspective, declaring during his confirmation hearing, "[I will] remember that it's my job to call balls and strikes, and not to pitch or bat." *Confirmation Hearing on the Nomination of John G. Roberts, Jr. to Be Chief Justice of the United States: Hearing Before the Senate Committee on the Judiciary*, 109th Cong. 56 (2005). Renowned judge Richard Posner, of the U.S. Court of Appeals for the Seventh Circuit, responded that the comment "was so ridiculous, and Chief Justice Roberts is so sophisticated, that it cannot be what he actually thought," noting that "judicial confirmation hearings have become a farce in which a display of candor would be suicide" (2010, 1181). For an empirical look at judicial nominee candor at the federal level, see Farganis and Wedeking 2011. Of course, recognizing that umpires and judges exercise considerable discretion can save the judge-as-umpire metaphor.

23. The literature on how judicial selection and retention institutions affect decision making is particularly voluminous (see also Brace and Hall 1997; Caldarone, Canes-Wrone, and Clark 2009; Canes-Wrone, Clark, and Park 2012; Melinda Gann Hall 1987; Hall and Brace 1992, 1996; Huber and Gordon 2004; Langer 2002; Shepherd 2009a, 2009b; Tabarrok and Helland 1999).

24. In *Republican Party of Minnesota v. White* (2002), the Court invalidated a state regulation prohibiting a candidate for judicial office from "announc[ing] his or her views on disputed legal or political issues" as a violation of the First Amendment's Free Speech Clause. Minn. Code of Judicial Conduct, Canon 5(A)(3)(d)(i) (2000). Scholars have found that the Court's decision in *White* did not result in normatively troubling consequences such as reduced citizen participation in judicial elections (Bonneau, Hall, and Streb 2011; Hall and Bonneau 2013).

In *Caperton v. A. T. Massey Coal Co.* (2009), the Court held that the Fourteenth Amendment's Due Process Clause requires recusal when "the probability of actual bias" moves beyond an unspecified threshold (2252). In doing so, the Court reversed a West Virginia Supreme Court ruling overturning a large jury verdict against a company whose CEO contributed more than $3 million to a state supreme court candidate while the case was pending appeal; that candidate ultimately defeated the incumbent, and the West Virginia Supreme Court later voted 3–2 (with the candidate in the majority) to overturn the jury verdict. Experimental evidence suggests that recusal is not a panacea for changes in perceptions of institutional legitimacy induced by campaign contributions (Gibson and Caldeira 2012). Moreover, survey evidence reveals that recusals do not fully restore the legitimacy-reducing effects of campaign activity (Gibson and Caldeira 2013). Related empirical evidence reveals that per se recusal rules are associated with decreases in certain large campaign donations (Miller and Curry 2013).

In *Williams-Yulee v. The Florida Bar* (2015), the Court held that a state bar rule prohibiting candidates for judicial office from personally soliciting campaign funds did not violate the First Amendment's Free Speech Clause. For predecision analyses of the issues involved in *Williams-Yulee*, see Bonneau and Redman 2015; Geyh 2015; and Ware 2015.

25. Specifically, Justice O'Connor (2014) favors merit selection as one part of the broader "O'Connor Judicial Selection Plan," which consists of "commission-based gubernatorial appointment of judges, with performance evaluation and periodic retention elections." Essentially, the O'Connor plan is a variation of the merit plan.

26. This information was compiled using Gavel to Gavel's database of state court legislation, at http://gaveltogavel.us/database. Specifically, for every bill coded by Gavel to Gavel as having to do with judicial selection, the short bill description was consulted to determine whether it involved merit selection or some other judicial selection institution (e.g., switching from nonpartisan to partisan elections).

27. Legislation proposing a switch from partisan to nonpartisan elections is an example of a bill that does not involve merit selection.

28. See the Constitution Reform Act 2005.

29. A discussion of the commission's procedures and responsibilities is available on the commission's website, at https://jac.judiciary.gov.uk/about-us.

30. For more on the Northern Ireland Judicial Appointments Commission, see its website, at http://www.nijac.gov.uk. For more on Scotland's Judicial Appointments Board, see its website, at http://www.judicialappointmentsscotland.org.uk/Home.

31. Although the procedural requirements for implementing reform were satisfied in late 2014, implementation was delayed to resolve pending lawsuits concerning the commission (Rajagopal 2015).

Chapter 2

1. England transferred judicial appointment authority from the lord chancellor to a Judicial Appointments Commission in 2005 (see Maute 2007). For a discussion of judicial selection systems in other countries, see Epstein, Knight, and Shvetsova 2001.

2. See Charter for the Province of Pennsylvania (1681), available at http://avalon.law.yale.edu/17th_century/pa01.asp. Connecticut and Rhode Island were exceptions, with both granting authority to establish courts legislatively in their original charters (Surrency 1967, 265).

3. See Resolution of the Continental Congress, Recommendation by the Congress to Establish Governments in the Several Colonies (May 15, 1776).

4. See Declaration of Independence (July 4, 1776).

5. Legislatures controlled judicial selection in Georgia, New Hampshire, New Jersey, North Carolina, and South Carolina. Judicial appointments were made by an executive council in Pennsylvania. Appointments were made by the governor with consent of a council in Maryland, New York, and Vermont. Delaware employed a joint ballot of the executive and legislature.

6. See Constitution of Vermont, Section 27 (July 8, 1777).

7. See Articles of Confederation, Section 9 (March 1, 1781). Section 9 of the Articles of Confederation also included a provision allowing Congress to appoint judges on an ad hoc basis to hear disputes between states if those states could not mutually agree on a panel of judges. The Articles of Confederation did not establish a U.S. Supreme Court.

8. For an overview of the process, see Goldman 1997.

9. See the Virginia Plan, Resolution 9 (1787), available at http://avalon.law .yale.edu/18th_century/vatexta.asp.

10. Alexander Hamilton, who personally favored unilateral appointment by the executive, had earlier proposed a plan calling for presidential appointment with Senate approval, although he did not explicitly mention judges (A. White 2005, 113).

11. See Constitution of the United States, Article II, Section 2 (1789).

12. Although political luminaries such as Thomas Jefferson and Andrew Jackson talked about the benefits of judicial elections (see Volcansek and Lafon 1988), neither made a serious push for them at the federal level. The subject of federal judicial elections has garnered some scholarly attention (e.g., R. Davis 2005; Zeisberg 2009). Of course, relatively minor institutional reforms regarding the federal judicial selection process have been made, including President Jimmy Carter's experimentation with merit panels and various changes in Senate filibuster rules. For discussion of reform to the length of tenure for U.S. Supreme Court justices, see Calabresi and Lindgren 2006.

13. Judges on Georgia's superior courts, which were the highest state courts at the time, were selected by the legislature. Georgia established a supreme court in 1845.

14. For case studies of the push toward judicial elections within particular states, see Klemme 2002 and Long 2002.

15. Experimental evidence suggests that party labels reduce abstention in judicial elections (Klein and Baum 2001).

16. Former chief justice of the Nebraska Supreme Court Norman Krivosha observes that "while [Pound's] speech alone may not have been sufficient to prompt Herbert Harley to induce Charles Ruggles to underwrite and establish the American Judicature Society in 1913, there is no doubt that Pound's words and the meanings contained therein played a significant role along with other factors then present" (1990, 128).

17. Kales (1914b) attributed the intellectual origins of his plan to a proposal of unknown origins granting state supreme court justices appointment power and a New Jersey plan allowing the chancellor of the court of chancery to appoint vice-chancellors to fixed terms.

18. The Louisiana Bar Association's plan also provided for what are now called retention elections. Thus, the proposal was an early version of the Missouri Plan.

19. In addition to Warren, the committee also included representatives from the California State Chamber of Commerce, California Federation of Women's Clubs, the state bar, legal community, and local police (M. Smith 1951, 579n59).

20. The plan is detailed in an introductory footnote of Gardner, Fisher, and Martin 1936–1937.

21. Responding to similar concerns about removing the people from the judicial selection process, some proposals began including provisions for citizen representation on commissions. In 1936, for example, the Michigan State Bar Association advanced a proposal for judicial selection based on gubernatorial appointment from a list of nominations supplied by a commission comprising three judges, three lawyers, and three lay persons—all of whom would be appointed by the governor with the advice and consent of the state senate (J. Wood 1937, 103). Glenn Winters (1968) traces the origins of proposals to include lay commission members to 1931.

22. Subsequently, voters in Clay, Greene, Platte, and St. Louis Counties adopted variations of the Missouri Plan as well.

23. In 1950, Alabama adopted a merit selection plan limited to interim appointments in Jefferson County, encompassing Birmingham (Shugerman 2012).

24. See, e.g., the minutes of the thirty-second day of the Alaska Constitutional Convention (December 9, 1955), available at http://www.law.state.ak.us/doclibrary/cc_minutes.html.

Chapter 3

1. This literature is related to a broader one on judges' professional experiences (see, e.g., Bonneau 2001; Fournet et al. 2009; K. Hall 1976a, 1976b, 1976c; Mott, Albright, and Semmerling 1933).

2. Notwithstanding a broad theoretical literature, comparatively little empirical analysis has been devoted to understanding the consequences of career homogeneity. This may be partly because of the difficulty inherent in measuring court-level experiential diversity. Recently, however, scholars have explored innovative ways to measure court-level experiential diversity that may aid in testing existing theoretical arguments (e.g., Barton and Moran 2013).

3. This remark was made during an appearance at Davidson College on March 12, 2015. A complete video of the appearance is available at http://www.davidson.edu/news/news-stories/150312-conversation-with-supreme-court-justice-sonia-sotomayor.

4. Former Pennsylvania governor Ed Rendell once argued, for example, that merit selection would "help ensure the most qualified individuals . . . even those without political connections . . . get appointed." See "Governor Rendell Endorses" 2009.

5. The Cook County Bar Association, for example, once argued against a proposed amendment to the Illinois Constitution to enact merit selection by declaring that such a system "encourage[d] cronyism and political favoritism" while disadvantaging "people who are not well-known or powerful" (Gofen 1987, 22).

6. Political economy is one field that devotes considerable attention to clarifying the concept of political connectedness. Nonetheless, creative measures for capturing the concept empirically often rely on specialized data that are not generalizable to a wide range of interdisciplinary applications (see, e.g., Fisman 2001).

7. Although nearly any professional position can be thought to enhance qualifications for the bench, judicial experience seems to be the only one that a substantial number of stakeholders consider something of a prerequisite for high court service.

8. Following other research in this area, I code public service experience in terms of a justice's previous employment. It is important to note, however, that many lawyers in private practice also engage in public service activities such as pro bono work and service on public interest boards (see Granfield and Mather 2009; Handler et al. 1975; Sandefur 2007).

9. That Brandeis himself came to be referred to as "the people's lawyer" while employed in private practice illustrates that the boundary between public service and private practice is not always clear. For a discussion of Brandeis's public interest activities while working in private practice, see, generally, Strum 1984, 54–73.

10. For an overview of the political positions held by U.S. Supreme Court justices, see Epstein et al. 2012.

11. There is a wealth of evidence that interpersonal dynamics on collegial courts help shape the development of law (see, e.g., Epstein and Knight 1997; Maltzman, Spriggs, and Wahlbeck 2000).

12. There is little empirical evidence on these questions.

13. Having held major political office is at best a noisy signal of the depth of political connections. Although it may be reasonable to assume that holding major political office means having strong political connections, not having this experience provides little information about the depth of one's political connections.

14. At the same time, Milliken filled another vacancy created by Justice Blair Moody Jr.'s death shortly after he was reelected to a new term in the November election. Although Milliken argued that newly appointed justice Dorothy Comstock Riley could fill out the remainder of the deceased justice's new term, the Michigan Supreme Court ultimately ruled (with Justice Brickley dissenting) that Riley was entitled to only the remainder of Moody's previous term, ending January 1, 1982. See *Attorney General v. Riley* (1983). In 1984, Riley was elected to the Michigan Supreme Court and served until 1997.

15. Although Kansas uses merit selection to fill supreme court vacancies, the governor now nominates lower court judges unilaterally. While Kansas formerly used merit selection to fill intermediate appellate court vacancies, the system was switched to unilateral gubernatorial appointment after the nominating commission failed to forward Stegall's name to the governor for an appellate court vacancy in 2012 (see Morris 2014).

16. Although state attorneys general regularly engage in litigation, they are "not considered prosecutors in the traditional sense" (Worrall 2008, 4). Nearly all chief local prosecutors are elected (see, e.g., Goelzhauser 2013; Gordon and Huber 2002; Wright 2009). U.S. attorneys are nominated by the president and confirmed by the Senate. However, these positions are often filled through senatorial courtesy.

17. In 2010, the Texas State Commission on Judicial Conduct charged Keller with several counts of misconduct stemming from in-office actions. Although Keller received a "public warning" about her conduct, this reprimand was overturned on appeal (Graczyk 2010). Keller was reelected in 2012.

18. *Miranda v. Arizona* (1966) is perhaps the best known of Warren's criminal procedure opinions. In *Miranda*, the Court held that the prosecution must demonstrate that procedural safeguards had been invoked to ensure that defendants understood the constitutional prohibition against compelled self-incrimination before relying on certain statements at trial.

19. Information on each justice's professional position immediately preceding appointment to the U.S. Supreme Court was obtained from Epstein et al. 2013.

20. Before joining the California Supreme Court, Liu had been nominated by President Barack Obama to fill a vacancy on the U.S. Court of Appeals for the Ninth Circuit (see Tobias 2013). The Senate successfully filibustered Liu's nomination, and Liu subsequently withdrew from consideration in 2011. He was nominated to the California Supreme Court about two months later.

21. All but one of the state supreme court justices with experience as full-time faculty members had at least a joint appointment in a law school. Victoria Lederberg is the exception. Lederberg, who also served in the Rhode Island House of Representatives, earned a Ph.D. in psychology from Brown and was a member of the Department of Psychology at Rhode Island College before entering law school and eventually becoming a justice on the Rhode Island Supreme Court.

22. Biographical information for these two justices noted that they served in major political offices, but there was not enough information to include them in calculations for the other categories.

23. Former Alabama Supreme Court chief justice Sue Bell Cobb does not appear to have had any pre-judicial experience. Cobb appears to have been appointed as a county district court judge after graduating from law school. Subsequently, Cobb was elected to the position in 1982 and served until she was elected to the Alabama Court of Appeals in 1994. In 2007, Cobb was elected to the Alabama Supreme Court, becoming its first female chief justice. Cobb resigned from the

Alabama Supreme Court in 2011 before the end of her term. See Alabama Department of Archives and History 2011.

24. Considerably more have part-time experience through adjunct teaching.

25. As discussed in Chapter 4, a majority of state supreme court justices also had prior judicial experience.

26. This variable combines justices seated by governors, legislators, and state supreme courts.

27. For example, Lisa Holmes (2012) analyzes the relationship between institutional rules and the decision to nominate and confirm federal judges with private practice experience.

28. Data on institutional rules through 2005 were obtained from the State Politics and the Judiciary Database compiled by Stefanie A. Lindquist. Subsequent years were updated using information provided by the American Judicature Society, at http://www.judicialselection.us. (Since the dissolution of the American Judicature Society, that information is now hosted by the National Center for State Courts.)

29. To avoid dropping observations with no state term limit in place, I set the number of years to twenty-six for these observations. This corresponds to the average number of terms served by U.S. Supreme Court justices who retired between 1970 and 2005 (Calabresi and Lindgren 2006, 771).

30. Data from 1990 and 2000 were obtained from the Census Bureau's Equal Employment Opportunity records. Data from 1980 were obtained from Hurwitz and Lanier 2003. Data for other years were extrapolated and interpolated from these values.

31. Specifically, I use a measure of state citizen ideology that varies over time (see Berry et al. 1998).

32. Region fixed effects are based on a nine-category census grouping available as part of the State Politics and the Judiciary Database.

33. These variables include time (a count variable increasing by one in each year of the sample period), time squared, and time cubed.

34. Predicted probabilities were calculated using SPost (Long and Freese 2006), setting binary variables at their modal values and other variables at their mean values. Values were rounded to the nearest nonzero whole number.

35. Including known voluntary merit selection plans yields an estimated coefficient that is not statistically distinguishable from zero at the 95 percent threshold.

36. Including known voluntary merit selection plans yields an estimated coefficient that is not statistically distinguishable from zero at the 95 percent threshold.

37. Including known voluntary merit selection plans yields a negative estimated coefficient on the election variable that is statistically distinguishable from zero at the 95 percent threshold, indicating that individuals with full-time academic experience are less likely on average to be seated by elections compared with merit selection.

38. Having held any elected office is another commonly used proxy for political connections (see, e.g., Carey 1998, 84; Hagopian 1994, 43; Krasno and Green 1988, 922). However, in the context of state judicial selection decisions, this measure is problematic for the same reason that the measures of holding major political office and having ties to major political office are problematic.

39. There is also a burgeoning literature on whether political donations to state supreme court justices influence their decision making (Cann 2007; Cann, Bonneau, and Boyea 2012; Shepherd 2009c).

40. Examples of prominent family connections among state supreme court justices in this sample include being a husband of a former state legislator (Brent Appel, Iowa), widow of a former state supreme court justice (Caroline Duby Glasman, Maine), son and son-in-law of former governors (Henry Mark Kennedy, Alabama), and grandson of a congressperson and son of a state senator (James Stephenson, Kentucky). Of course, these ties are not necessarily evidence that the individuals were not qualified for their positions. Instead, the examples simply illustrate the types of connections that might be of interest to anyone interested in developing better measures to capture the contested concept.

41. Of course, political connections and family ties are also likely to be endogenous to characteristics such as work experience that are thought to be important. There is not likely to be a panacea for capturing political connections empirically given the diversity of ways that they can arise and become influential. One example illustrates the problem. After I. Beverly Lake Sr. lost an initial primary in North Carolina's 1968 gubernatorial race, he publicly supported his friend Dan Moore's candidacy in exchange for Moore's promise to appoint Lake to the North Carolina Supreme Court if he became governor; Moore ultimately won the election at least in part because of Lake's support and subsequently appointed Lake to the North Carolina Supreme Court with his first opportunity (Covington and Ellis 1999, 355). Generating a reasonably precise and general ex ante definition of political connections that accounts for an anecdote like this and can be captured empirically is a difficult task. This difficulty may be particularly pressing when it comes to accounting for connections based on friendship. Like Lake, several justices in the sample had prominent friends. In 1980, for example, Minnesota governor Albert Quie, known for "his great leadership on merit selection" in the state (Boyd 2013, 673), appointed John Simonett to the Minnesota Supreme Court following Walter Rogosheske's retirement. Rogosheske and Simonett were friends and next-door neighbors, and Rogosheske encouraged Simonett to apply for the vacancy his retirement created (Boyd 2013, 672). Simonett had also been a friend and law partner of Gorden Rosenmeier, a state senator described as "the most powerful politician in Minnesota between 1940 and 1970" (Anderson 2013, 682).

42. Firm information is available for some of the most recent seatings. However, this information by itself is of limited use for two reasons. First, justices might have worked at a firm a long time ago, and the current firm, if it still exists, might have changed considerably. Second, and perhaps more problematically, many firms cover a range of practice areas, and which areas the justice practiced in are often not clear.

Chapter 4

1. The brief discussion about judicial qualifications occurred on June 5, 1787, and is reported in James Madison's notes, which are available at http://avalon.law .yale.edu/subject_menus/debcont.asp.

2. Although it is sometimes said that Franklin proposed nomination by lawyers as the preferred method of selecting federal judges, James Madison's notes merely suggest that he wanted further discussion on the subject and relayed the Scottish anecdote "in a brief and entertaining manner." See the notes of June 5, 1787.

3. See Madison's notes of June 5, 1787.

4. The ABA discusses these criteria in its manual titled *American Bar Association Standing Committee on the Federal Judiciary: What It Is and How It Works* (2009). The success of the ABA in infusing the nomination process with merit is unclear. While ABA ratings are associated with merit-related factors such as judicial experience, they may also be biased with respect to ideology, gender, and race (Haire 2001; Sen 2014; Smelcer, Steigerwalt, and Vining 2012).

5. Exec. Order No. 11,972 (February 14, 1977).

6. Exec. Order No. 12,097 (November 8, 1978).

7. For a detailed discussion of Wisconsin's Federal Nominating Commission, which has been in use since 1979, see A. Owens 2005.

8. Even those who argued against judicial elections often agreed that the people were well suited to select qualified judges. As one delegate to the Massachusetts Convention explained, "I am opposed to an elective judiciary system, but not because the people are not competent to elect a good bench. I believe they are" (*Official Report* 1853, 413).

9. The November 1953 proceedings of the Nebraska State Bar Association's annual meeting, published in the *Nebraska Law Review*, refer to Laurens Williams introducing the phrase. See "Proceedings" 1953, 186. The first use of the phrase in writing seems to be in an article titled "The President's Message," delivered by Williams in the *Nebraska State Bar Journal*, where he wrote, "In the referendum conducted a little over a year ago on the Merit Plan for the Selection and Tenure of Judges (formerly called the 'Missouri Plan') the members of the Association voted 933 in favor, 380 against the Plan, and mandated the Association officers to get a Constitutional Amendment on the ballot in 1954" (L. Williams 1953, 8).

10. In addition to these literatures, there is also evidence that judicial qualifications influence decisions about whom to vote for (Baum 1987) and the share of votes received (Bonneau and Hall 2009) in judicial elections.

11. In merit plan states, the selection and retention mechanisms are perfectly correlated by definition. In general, merit selection tends to be paired with retention elections, but there are exceptions, as noted in Chapter 1.

12. For example, a member of the *New Jersey Star-Ledger* editorial board once wrote that New Jersey Supreme Court nominee Bruce Harris "went to elite schools, graduating from Yale Law School in 1992, so there's no doubt he's a smart guy" (Moran 2012). New Jersey's Senate Judiciary Committee ultimately rejected

Harris's nomination. Of course, one need not agree with the assumption to acknowledge that it is a heuristic to which many subscribe.

13. A discussion of changes to the ranking system is available on the *Prelaw Handbook* website, at http://www.prelawhandbook.com/law_school_ranking__usn_history.

14. Whereas Sen (2014) used information from the 2001 rankings, I use the 2004 rankings.

15. In alphabetical order, these schools are Berkeley, Chicago, Columbia, Cornell, Duke, Georgetown, Harvard, Michigan, New York University, Northwestern, Penn, Stanford, Virginia, and Yale.

16. Adam Chilton and Eric Posner, for example, "decided to define elite law schools as the Top-14 law schools in the *U.S. News and World Report* Rankings because it is the definition common[ly] used in both academic scholarship and discourse more widely" (2014, 7).

17. Categories are based on the 2004 *U.S. News and World Report*'s law school rankings, available on the Prelaw Handbook website, at http://www.prelawhandbook.com/law_school_rankings__2000_present.

18. Some states did not have public (or any) law schools during the sample period. Condition 3 was captured using the 2004 *U.S. News and World Report* rankings. Examples of condition 3 being satisfied include a justice on the Missouri Supreme Court having attended Washington University rather than the University of Missouri at Columbia and a justice on the Tennessee Supreme Court having attended Vanderbilt rather than the University of Tennessee. As a robustness check, I fit a model replacing condition 3 with a coding rule that included graduating from any law school ranked higher than the state's flagship law school. The results are substantively similar.

19. Including information on whether a state supreme court justice served a judicial clerkship after graduation yields substantively similar results, although the estimated coefficient for the elections variable attains statistical significance only at the 90 percent threshold. Judicial clerkships are prestigious positions that generally signal a high level of aptitude and performance in law school. Clerk responsibilities may include conducting background research on pending cases, reviewing and offering recommendations about whether to grant motions or review appeals, and drafting orders and opinions (see, e.g., Peppers 2006; Peppers and Ward 2012; Ward and Weiden 2006). The origins of the Supreme Court clerkship date back to Justice Horace Gray in the late nineteenth century. But Justice Gray also employed law clerks during his time on the Massachusetts Supreme Court from 1873 through 1882 (Peppers 2007, 231). In general, however, the clerkship institution did not begin to steadily spread at all three levels of the federal judiciary and in state courts until the second quarter of the twentieth century (see, e.g., Baier 1973; Peppers, Giles, and Tainer-Parkins 2008; Posner 1999, 139–159). As a result, I do not include information on clerkship experience in the main results presented in this chapter.

20. One potential limitation with the law review indicator is that it does not account for law review membership presumably being more difficult to obtain as the average quality of the student body increases. Thus, one might object that the measure disfavors students who attend better schools. There are two responses to this objection. First, this point would hold regardless of which measure of academic performance one chooses. Second, difference in school quality is accounted for in the other measures used here. Moreover, academic performance is conceptually distinct from law school quality. As a proxy for academic performance specifically, the objection carries less weight.

21. Applications in several other states often have a section devoted to law school honors, where law review service can be listed.

22. Although one might think that executives who are lawyers may be more likely to mention such a distinction (see Blackstone and Goelzhauser 2014), non-lawyer executives mention it as well. During Brett Kavanaugh's swearing-in ceremony to the U.S. Court of Appeals for the D.C. Circuit, for example, President George W. Bush noted that Kavanaugh "was an editor of the Yale Law Review" (Bush 2006, 1064).

23. The appellate experience variable is scored only for individuals in states with an intermediate appellate court.

24. Percentages do not add up to 100 because of rounding.

25. A Brant test revealed that the parallel regression assumption is violated when fitting the ordinal law school ranking model with ordered logit. Fitting the model with ordinal generalized linear regression (R. Williams 2010) yielded similar results.

26. The number of observations differs across models for several reasons. First, not every justice in the sample graduated from law school. Justices who did not graduate from law school were coded zero in the elite and locally elite law school models because they did not graduate from the relevant schools. These justices are excluded from the ordinal law school rankings model, however, because sorting into a category requires having graduated from law school. Second, background information for some justices in the database could not be located. Many of the missing observations on the academic performance indicator arose because some law schools did not have law reviews at the time a justice graduated; in other instances, mastheads, which list law review members for each volume or issue, could not be located. The appellate experience model includes observations only from states with intermediate appellate courts. The years of experience variables account for justices seated from 2000 through 2014.

27. Quantities of interest were calculated using SPost (Long and Freese 2006), setting binary variables at their modal values and other variables at their mean values. Values were rounded to the nearest nonzero whole number.

28. In addition, including known voluntary merit selection plans yields a negative estimated coefficient on the elections variable that is statistically distinguishable from zero at the 95 percent threshold, indicating that individuals who

attended lower-ranked law schools are less likely to be seated on average under elections relative to merit selection.

Chapter 5

1. One judge argues, "A diverse judiciary signals the public acknowledgment of historically excluded communities and sends an invaluable message of inclusion. It enhances courts' credibility among affected communities who would otherwise feel they have no voice within the institution. It helps dispel traditional stereotypes that . . . minorities are not sufficiently intelligent, articulate, or decisive to be judges. And it assures students and young lawyers from historically underrepresented communities that they need not limit their aspirations" (Chen 2003, 1117).

2. Overall, the empirical results on the link between race and judicial decision making are mixed (see, e.g., Farhang and Wawro 2004; Scherer 2005; Welch, Combs, and Gruhl 1988).

3. As with the studies on race and substantive representation, the results on gender and substantive representation are mixed (see, e.g., Gryski, Main, and Dixon 1986; Martin and Pyle 2005; Songer, Davis, and Haire 1994).

4. For an earlier qualitative approach to examining whether female and male judges approach opinion writing differently, see S. Davis 1992.

5. Female state supreme court justices are also more likely to publish dissenting opinions in cases that involve women's issues (Szmer, Christensen, and Kaheny 2015).

6. An Illinois trial judge did, however, admit Kepley to practice (Chused 2003, 425n22).

7. The Fourteenth Amendment's Privileges or Immunities Clause reads, "No State shall make or enforce any law which shall abridge the privileges or immunities of citizens of the United States." U.S. Constitution, Amendment 14, Section 1.

8. Chief Justice Edward G. Ryan's opinion for the Wisconsin Supreme Court denying Goodell admission to the bar was widely praised in legal circles. The *San Francisco Law Journal*, for example, prefaced its reproduction of the portion of the opinion quoted here by declaring, "There is so much in it that is wise, truthful, and earnest, so much that is logical, learned, and beautiful, so much that is tender and respectful, so much that is legal and practical, that we have felt compelled to give space for its publication" (Baggett 1878, 50). In 1878, the Wisconsin legislature passed a law prohibiting gender discrimination in bar admissions, and Goodell ultimately became the first woman admitted to practice in the state when the Wisconsin Supreme Court upheld the law over Chief Justice Ryan's silent dissent (*In re Goodell* [1879]). Nonetheless, forty years later a subsequent chief justice of the Wisconsin Supreme Court quoted from Ryan's opinion at length in an article on the gradual transfer of property rights to married women, noting that his predecessor had "gilded the bitter pill [to Goodell] with that inimitable felicity of language which was all his own" (Winslow 1917, 55–56) and praising "the elevation of the thought and the beauty, not to say the majesty, of the diction" (57).

9. It has been widely reported that Rehnquist finished first in the class and O'Connor third. However, Stanford does not seem to have ranked students from top to bottom (see Montini 2005). Nonetheless, it is clear that O'Connor and Rehnquist were at the top of their class because both were selected to serve on the *Stanford Law Review* and join the Order of the Coif. See, e.g., Stanford News Service 2005.

10. H.R.J. Res. No. 208, 92d Cong., 2d Sess. (1972). After being introduced in Congress a few years after the Nineteenth Amendment's ratification, the ERA was reintroduced in every Congress from 1923 until it was proposed in 1972 (Ginsburg 1973, 1013).

11. This language reflects what the U.S. Supreme Court calls "intermediate scrutiny." In *Frontiero v. Richardson* (1973), four justices advocated subjecting gender-based classifications to "strict scrutiny," an even higher burden for the government that would have required it to demonstrate that the classification was motivated by a compelling government interest and was narrowly tailored to achieve that interest. For an analysis of how political factors shaped the Court's decision making with respect to the appropriate level of scrutiny, including a consideration of the ERA's influence, see B. Friedman 2009, 289–295.

12. Although the Fourteenth Amendment explicitly applies to states, the equal protection principle limits the federal government through reverse incorporation with the Fifth Amendment's Due Process Clause. See, e.g., *Bolling v. Sharpe* (1954). For more on the continued use of reverse incorporation, see Primus 2004.

13. Genevieve Rose Cline became the first female federal judge when she was appointed to the U.S. Customs Court by President Coolidge in 1928 (Cedarbaum 1993, 40).

14. After the Wyoming Territory enfranchised women in 1869, Esther Morris became the first female judge in the country when she was named a justice of the peace in South Pass City, Wyoming (Karin 2004). For a list of the first female judges in every state, see Berkson 1982, 290.

15. The Reconstruction Amendments include the Thirteenth Amendment (abolishing slavery; ratified in 1865), Fourteenth Amendment (addressing citizenship and prohibiting states from denying or abridging privileges or immunities, due process, or the equal protection of the laws; ratified in 1868), and Fifteenth Amendment (prohibiting states from denying voting rights to males on the basis of race; ratified in 1870). For a detailed history of the Reconstruction Amendments, see Richards 1993. For a detailed history of Jim Crow laws, see Woodward 2002.

16. The Fourteenth Amendment's Equal Protection Clause reads, "Nor [shall any state] deny to any person within its jurisdiction the equal protection of the laws." U.S. Constitution, Amendment 14, Section 1.

17. Langston went on to serve in a variety of important positions, including as founder and dean of Howard University Law School and member of the U.S. House of Representatives (Langston 1894).

18. In 1939, Lloyd Gaines, whose application for admission to the University of Missouri School of Law set in motion events leading to the U.S. Supreme

Court's decision in *Missouri ex rel. Gaines,* went missing, and the mystery of his disappearance remains unsolved (Garrison 2007). In *Sipuel v. Board of Regents of the University of Oklahoma* (1948), decided a decade later, the U.S. Supreme Court held that a state must provide legal education for black students if it provided legal education for white students.

19. Other major cases eroded *Plessy's* separate but equal rule as well during this period. In *McLaurin v. Oklahoma State Regents for Higher Education* (1950), for example, the U.S. Supreme Court held that black students admitted to a university could not be subject to certain discriminatory regulations. Before bringing suit, the plaintiff, a black graduate student at the University of Oklahoma, had been "required to sit apart at a designated desk in an anteroom adjoining the classroom; to sit at a designated desk on the mezzanine floor of the library, but not to use the desks in the regular reading room; and to sit at a designated table and to eat at a different time from the other students in the school cafeteria" (640).

20. Hastie took the position in 1949 as a recess appointment and was confirmed in 1950. Previously, Hastie had also become the first black federal judge when he served a fixed term as a district court judge in the Virgin Islands (Rusch 1978, 803n340).

21. These states were Alaska, Arizona, Delaware, Hawaii, Idaho, Iowa, Kansas, Maine, Montana, Nebraska, New Hampshire, New Mexico, North Dakota, Oregon, Rhode Island, South Dakota, Utah, Vermont, and Wyoming.

22. Marumoto had been appointed to the Supreme Court of the Territory of Hawaii by President Eisenhower. He was the only member of that court to be appointed to the Hawaii Supreme Court in 1959 (see Quinn 1960, 91).

23. Although post-Carter presidents emphasized judicial diversity to different extents (see, e.g., Goldman 1989; Solberg 2005; Spill and Bratton 2000), the issue became entrenched on the federal political agenda following Carter. President Carter's efforts were aided by the creation of more than a hundred new judgeships and a push to diversify political institutions more generally (see, e.g., M. Clark 2002, 2011; Cook 1984; Ginsburg and Brill 1995).

24. In addition to multistate studies, there have been numerous state-specific studies (e.g., Dubois 1983; Hurwitz 2010; Lanier and Handberg 2011; K. Myers 2013; Salokar, Berggren, and DePalo 2006; Tokarz 1986; Yelnosky 2010). For a variety of diversity-related statistics on the internal workings of certain merit commissions, see Esterling and Andersen 1999.

25. When state supreme and intermediate appellate judges were pooled, however, the authors found that elite nomination (without a commission) was associated with a decrease in the number of female judges (Hurwitz and Lanier 2003).

26. I supplemented this approach by searching for information about the number of political minority justices for each state. For example, if publicly available information noted that a state seated its first black justice in 1990, justices seated previously were coded as nonblack. Although biographical information on some justices in the database was not available, this approach allowed me to code information about gender and race for each justice in the database.

27. The number of Hispanic and Asian American state supreme court justices is still quite low, necessitating combining them in a single model to avoid over-fitting.

28. The percentage of seats filled by political minorities does not reflect the aggregate percentage of individuals in specific categories because some justices are counted in more than one group. Although intersectionality has not been the subject of much research with respect to state courts, it has received some attention at the federal level (see, e.g., Collins and Moyer 2008).

29. Census data on the number of Asian American lawyers in a state were not available for the same periods. Thus, the data for nonblack lawyers combine the number of Asian American and Hispanic lawyers in a state.

30. Quantities of interest were calculated using SPost (Long and Freese 2006), setting binary variables at their modal values and other variables at their mean values. Values were rounded to the nearest nonzero whole number.

31. Including known voluntary merit selection plans yields a negative estimated coefficient on the elections variable that is statistically distinguishable from zero at the 95 percent threshold, indicating that political minorities are less likely to be seated on average under elections relative to merit selection.

Chapter 6

1. For an overview of open questions concerning the operation of commission-based selection systems, see Tarr 2007.

2. Examples of these minimum qualifications include requirements that a judge have reached a certain age and have been licensed to practice in the state for some number of years.

REFERENCES

Abel, Richard L. 1985. "Law without Politics: Legal Aid under Advanced Capitalism." *UCLA Law Review* 32 (3): 474–642.

"About Phil Johnson." n.d. *Justice Phil Johnson.* Available at http://www.justice philjohnson.com/#about (accessed October 14, 2015).

Abraham, Henry J. 2008. *Justices, Presidents, and Senators: A History of the U.S. Supreme Court Appointments from Washington to Bush II.* 5th ed. Lanham, MD: Rowman and Littlefield.

Alabama Department of Archives and History. 2011. "Alabama's Supreme Court Chief Justices: Sue Bell Cobb." Available at http://www.archives.alabama.gov/judicial/cobb.html.

Alleman, Robert, and Jason Mazzone. 2010. "The Case for Returning Politicians to the Supreme Court." *Hastings Law Journal* 61 (6): 1353–1406.

Alozie, Nicholas O. 1988. "Black Representation on State Judiciaries." *Social Science Quarterly* 69 (4): 979–986.

———. 1990. "Distribution of Women and Minority Judges: The Effects of Judicial Selection Methods." *Social Science Quarterly* 71 (2): 315–325.

———. 1996. "Selection Methods and the Recruitment of Women to State Courts of Last Resort." *Social Science Quarterly* 77 (1): 110–126.

American Bar Association. 2009. *American Bar Association Standing Committee on the Federal Judiciary: What It Is and How It Works.* Chicago: American Bar Association.

American Judicature Society. n.d. "Merit Selection: The Best Way to Choose the Best Judges." Available at http://www.judicialselection.us/uploads/docu ments/ms_descrip_1185462202120.pdf (accessed September 9, 2015).

Anderson, Douglas P. 2013. "Boss, Mentor, and Friend." *William Mitchell Law Review* 39 (3): 682–684.

Ashenfelter, Orley, Theodore Eisenberg, and Stewart J. Schwab. 1995. "Politics and the Judiciary: The Influence of Judicial Background on Case Outcomes." *Journal of Legal Studies* 24 (2): 257–281.

Attorney General v. Riley, 417 Mich. 119 (1983).

Aumann, Francis R. 1940. *The Changing American Legal System: Some Selected Phases.* Columbus: Ohio State University Press.

Baggett, W. T., ed. 1878. "Notes." *San Francisco Law Journal* 1 (4): 49–64.

Baier, Paul R. 1973. "Law Clerks: Profile of an Institution." *Vanderbilt Law Review* 26 (6): 1125–1178.

Baldez, Lisa, Lee Epstein, and Andrew D. Martin. 2006. "Does the U.S. Constitution Need an Equal Rights Amendment?" *Journal of Legal Studies* 35 (1): 243–283.

Barnes, Robert, and Jennifer Agiesta. 2010. "Poll Affirms a Vote for Judicial Know-How." *Washington Post,* April 30. Available at http://www.washingtonpost.com/wp-dyn/content/article/2010/04/29/AR2010042904893.html.

Bartels, Brandon L., and Chris W. Bonneau, eds. 2015. *Making Law and Courts Research Relevant: The Normative Implications of Empirical Research.* New York: Routledge.

Barton, Benjamin H. 2012. "An Empirical Study of Supreme Court Justice Preappointment Experience." *Florida Law Review* 64 (5): 1137–1187.

Barton, Benjamin H., and Emily Moran. 2013. "Measuring Diversity on the Supreme Court with Biodiversity Statistics." *Journal of Empirical Legal Studies* 10 (1): 1–34.

Baum, Lawrence. 1987. "Explaining the Vote in Judicial Elections: The 1984 Ohio Supreme Court Elections." *Western Political Quarterly* 40 (2): 361–371.

Baye, Rachel. 2014. "Donors, Friends of Governors Often Get State Supreme Court Nod." Center for Public Integrity, May 1. Available at http://www.publicintegrity.org/2014/05/01/14692/donors-friends-governors-often-get-state-supreme-court-nod.

Bell, Derrick A., Jr. 1970. "Black Students in White Law Schools: The Ordeal and the Opportunity." *University of Toledo Law Review* 2 (2–3): 539–558.

Bell, John. 2003. "European Perspectives on a Judicial Appointments Commission." *Cambridge Yearbook of European Legal Studies* 6:35–54.

Benesh, Sara C. 2006. "Understanding Public Confidence in American Courts." *Journal of Politics* 68 (3): 697–707.

Berkson, Larry. 1982. "Women on the Bench: A Brief History." *Judicature* 65 (6): 286–292.

Berry, William D., Evan J. Ringquist, Richard C. Fording, and Russell L. Hanson. 1998. "Measuring Citizen and Government Ideology in the American States." *American Journal of Political Science* 42 (1): 327–348.

Bierman, Luke. 2002. "Beyond Merit Selection." *Fordham Urban Law Review* 29 (3): 851–872.

Bishop, William G., and William H. Attree. 1846. *Report of the Debates and Proceedings of the Convention for the Revision of the Constitution of the State of New York*. Albany, NY: Evening Atlas.

Blackmar, Charles B. 2007. "Missouri's Nonpartisan Court Plan from 1942 to 2005." *Missouri Law Review* 72 (1): 199–219.

Blackstone, Bethany, and Greg Goelzhauser. 2014. "Presidential Rhetoric toward the Supreme Court." *Judicature* 97 (4): 179–187.

Blackstone, William. 1759. *Commentaries on the Laws of England*. Vol. 1. Oxford: Clarendon.

Bobo, Lawrence, and Franklin D. Gilliam Jr. 1990. "Race, Sociopolitical Participation, and Black Empowerment." *American Political Science Review* 84 (2): 377–393.

Bolling v. Sharpe, 347 U.S. 497 (1954).

Bonica, Adam, Adam S. Chilton, and Maya Sen. 2015. "The Political Ideologies of American Lawyers." *Social Science Research Network*, August 26. Available at http://papers.ssrn.com/sol3/papers.cfm?abstract_id=2652706.

Bonica, Adam, and Michael J. Woodruff. 2015. "A Common-Space Measure of State Supreme Court Ideology." *Journal of Law, Economics, and Organization* 31 (3): 472–498.

Bonneau, Chris W. 2001. "The Composition of State Supreme Courts, 2000." *Judicature* 85 (1): 26–31.

———. 2004. "Patterns of Campaign Spending and Electoral Competition in State Supreme Court Elections." *Justice System Journal* 25 (1): 21–38.

———. 2005. "What Price Justice(s)? Understanding Campaign Spending in State Supreme Court Elections." *State Politics and Policy Quarterly* 5 (2): 107–125.

———. 2007. "The Effects of Campaign Spending in State Supreme Court Elections." *Political Research Quarterly* 60 (3): 489–499.

Bonneau, Chris W., and Damon M. Cann. 2011. "Campaign Spending, Diminishing Marginal Returns, and Campaign Finance Restrictions in Judicial Elections." *Journal of Politics* 73 (4): 1267–1280.

———. 2015a. "Party Identification and Vote Choice in Partisan and Nonpartisan Elections." *Political Behavior* 37 (1): 43–66.

———. 2015b. *Voters' Verdicts: Citizens, Campaigns, and Institutions in State Supreme Court Elections*. Charlottesville: University of Virginia Press.

Bonneau, Chris W., and Melinda Gann Hall. 2003. "Predicting Challengers in State Supreme Court Elections: Context and the Politics of Institutional Design." *Political Research Quarterly* 56 (3): 337–349.

———. 2009. *In Defense of Judicial Elections*. New York: Routledge.

Bonneau, Chris W., Melinda Gann Hall, and Matthew J. Streb. 2011. "*White* Noise: The Unrealized Effects of *Republican Party of Minnesota v. White* on Judicial Elections." *Justice System Journal* 32 (3): 247–268.

Bonneau, Chris W., and Eric Loepp. 2014. "Getting Things Straight: The Effects of Ballot Design and Electoral Structure on Voter Participation." *Electoral Studies* 34:119–130.

Bonneau, Chris W., and Shane M. Redman. 2015. "Much Ado about Nothing: The Irrelevance of *Williams-Yulee v. The Florida Bar* on the Conduct of Judicial Elections." *Vanderbilt Law Review En Banc* 68:31–41.

Bonneau, Chris W., and Heather Marie Rice. 2009. "Impartial Judges? Race, Institutional Context, and U.S. State Supreme Courts." *State Politics and Policy Quarterly* 9 (4): 381–403.

Bopp, James, Jr. 2013. "The Perils of Merit Selection." *Indiana Law Review* 46 (1): 87–102.

Borreca, Richard. 2007. "Senate Rejects Lingle Choice: Some Say That Judge Randall Lee Is a Victim of Political Payback." *Star Bulletin*, October 31. Available at http://archives.starbulletin.com/2007/10/31/news/story02.html.

Boyd, Christina L., Lee Epstein, and Andrew D. Martin. 2010. "Untangling the Causal Effects of Sex on Judging." *American Journal of Political Science* 54 (2): 389–411.

Boyd, Thomas H. 2013. "Foreword: The Distinguished Life and Work of the Honorable John E. Simonett." *William Mitchell Law Review* 39 (3): 666–681.

Boyea, Brent D. 2007. "Linking Judicial Selection to Consensus: An Analysis of Ideological Diversity." *American Politics Research* 35 (5): 643–670.

———. 2010. "Does Seniority Matter? The Conditional Influence of State Methods of Judicial Retention." *Social Science Quarterly* 91 (1): 209–227.

———. 2011. "Time Served in State Supreme Courts: Mapping the Determinants of Judicial Seniority." *Justice System Journal* 32 (1): 44–61.

Brace, Paul, and Brent D. Boyea. 2008. "State Public Opinion, the Death Penalty, and the Practice of Electing Judges." *American Journal of Political Science* 52 (2): 360–372.

Brace, Paul, and Melinda Gann Hall. 1990. "Neo-institutionalism and Dissent in State Supreme Courts." *Journal of Politics* 52 (1): 54–70.

———. 1993. "Integrated Models of Judicial Dissent." *Journal of Politics* 55 (4): 914–935.

———. 1997. "The Interplay of Preferences, Case Facts, Context, and Rules in the Politics of Judicial Choice." *Journal of Politics* 59 (4): 1206–1231.

———. 2001. "'Haves' versus 'Have Nots' in State Supreme Courts: Allocating Docket Space and Wins in Power Asymmetric Cases." *Law and Society Review* 35 (2): 393–417.

Brace, Paul, Melinda Gann Hall, and Laura Langer. 2001. "Placing State Supreme Courts in State Politics." *State Politics and Policy Quarterly* 1 (1): 81–108.

Bradwell v. Illinois, 83 U.S. 130 (1873).

Brandeis, Louis D. 1905. "The Opportunity in the Law." *American Law Review* 39 (4): 555–563.

Bratton, Kathleen A., and Rorie L. Spill. 2002. "Existing Diversity and Judicial Selection: The Role of the Appointment Method in Establishing Gender Diversity in State Supreme Courts." *Social Science Quarterly* 83 (2): 504–518.

Breyer, Stephen. 2000. "The Legal Profession and Public Service." *New York University Annual Survey of American Law* 57 (4): 403–418.

Broockman, David E. 2014. "Do Female Politicians Empower Women to Vote or Run for Office? A Regression Discontinuity Approach." *Electoral Studies* 34:190–204.

Brown, Gary S. 1996. "The Merits of Merit Selection." *Metropolitan Corporate Counsel*, May, p. 53.

Brown v. Board of Education, 347 U.S. 483 (1954).

Bundschu, Henry A. 1948. "The Missouri Non-partisan Court Plan: Selection and Tenure of Judges." *University of Kansas City Law Review* 16 (2): 55–67.

Bush, George W. 2006. "Remarks at a Swearing-In Ceremony for Brett Kavanaugh as a United States Circuit Judge for the District of Columbia." *Weekly Compilation of Presidential Documents* 42 (22): 1064–1065. Available at http://www.gpo.gov/fdsys/pkg/WCPD-2006-06-05/pdf/WCPD-2006-06-05-Pg1064.pdf.

Calabresi, Steven G., and James Lindgren. 2006. "Term Limits for the Supreme Court: Life Tenure Reconsidered." *Harvard Journal of Law and Public Policy* 29 (3): 769–877.

Caldarone, Richard P., Brandice Canes-Wrone, and Tom S. Clark. 2009. "Partisan Labels and Democratic Accountability: An Analysis of State Supreme Court Abortion Decisions." *Journal of Politics* 71 (2): 560–573.

Calder, Amy. 2009. "Colleagues, Friends Praise High Court Nominee; Superior Court Justice Joseph Jabar Would Replace Retiring Justice Robert Clifford." *Portland Press Herald*, August 5, p. B2.

Cane, Barbara H. 1981. "The Role of Law Review in Legal Education." *Journal of Legal Education* 31 (1): 215–232.

Canes-Wrone, Brandice, Tom S. Clark, and Jason P. Kelly. 2014. "Judicial Selection and Death Penalty Decisions." *American Political Science Review* 108 (1): 23–39.

Canes-Wrone, Brandice, Tom S. Clark, and Jee-Kwang Park. 2012. "Judicial Independence and Retention Elections." *Journal of Law, Economics, and Organization* 28 (2): 211–234.

Cann, Damon M. 2006. "Beyond Accountability and Independence: Judicial Selection and State Court Performance." *Judicature* 90 (5): 226–232.

———. 2007. "Justice for Sale? Campaign Contributions and Judicial Decision-making." *State Politics and Policy Quarterly* 7 (3): 281–297.

Cann, Damon M., Chris W. Bonneau, and Brent D. Boyea. 2012. "Campaign Contributions and Judicial Decisions in Partisan and Nonpartisan Elections." In *New Directions in Judicial Politics*, edited by Kevin T. McGuire, 38–52. New York: Routledge.

Cann, Damon M., and Teena Wilhelm. 2011. "Case Visibility and the Electoral Connection in State Supreme Courts." *American Politics Research* 39 (3): 557–581.

Cann, Damon M., and Jeff Yates. 2007. "Homegrown Institutional Legitimacy: Assessing Citizens' Diffuse Support for State Courts." *American Politics Research* 36 (2): 297–329.

Canon, Bradley C. 1972. "The Impact of Formal Selection Processes on the Characteristics of Judges—Reconsidered." *Law and Society Review* 6 (4): 579–594.

Caperton v. A.T. Massey Coal Co., 129 S. Ct. 2242 (2009).

Carey, John M. 1998. *Term Limits and Legislature Representation.* New York: Cambridge University Press.

Carter, David B., and Curtis S. Signorino. 2010. "Back to the Future: Modeling Time Dependence in Binary Data." *Political Analysis* 18 (3): 271–292.

Case, David W. 1992. "In Search of an Independent Judiciary: Alternatives to Judicial Elections in Mississippi." *Mississippi College Law Review* 13 (1): 1–36.

Caufield, Rachel Paine. 2007. "How the Pickers Pick: Finding a Set of Best Practices for Judicial Nominating Commissions." *Fordham Urban Law Journal* 34 (1): 163–202.

———. 2010. "What Makes Merit Selection Different." *Roger Williams University Law Review* 15 (3): 765–792.

———. 2011. "The Curious Logic of Judicial Elections." *Arkansas Law Review* 64 (1): 249–280.

———. 2012. *Inside Merit Selection: A National Survey of Judicial Nominating Commissioners.* Des Moines, IA: American Judicature Society.

Cedarbaum, Miriam Goldman. 1993. "Women on the Federal Bench." *Boston University Law Review* 73 (1): 39–45.

"Changing the Way We Select Judges." 2002. *Chicago Tribune,* March 8. Available at http://articles.chicagotribune.com/2002-03-08/news/0203080254_1_merit-selection-diversity-issue-hispanics.

Charles, Guy-Uriel E., Daniel L. Chen, and G. Mitu Gulati. 2011. "'Not That Smart': Sonia Sotomayor and the Construction of Merit." *Social Science Research Network,* August 17. Available at http://papers.ssrn.com/sol3/papers.cfm?abstract_id=1907724.

Chen, Edward M. 2003. "The Judiciary, Diversity, and Justice for All." *California Law Review* 91 (4): 1109–1124.

Chew, Pat K., and Luke T. Kelley-Chew. 2010. "The Missing Minority Judges." *Journal of Gender, Race and Justice* 14 (1): 179–198.

Chilton, Adam S., and Eric A. Posner. 2014. "An Empirical Study of Political Bias in Legal Scholarship." University of Chicago Coase-Sandor Institute for Law and Economics Working Paper no. 696. Available at http://chicagounbound.uchicago.edu/cgi/viewcontent.cgi?article=2376&context=law_and_economics.

Choi, Stephen J., Mitu Gulati, Mirya Holman, and Eric A. Posner. 2011. "Judging Women." *Journal of Empirical Legal Studies* 8 (3): 504–532.

Choi, Stephen J., G. Mitu Gulati, and Eric A. Posner. 2010. "Professionals or Politicians: The Uncertain Empirical Case for an Elected Rather than Appointed Judiciary." *Journal of Law, Economics, and Organization* 26 (2): 290–336.

Chused, Richard H. 2003. "A Brief History of Gender Law Journals: The Heritage of Myra Bradwell's Chicago Legal News." *Columbia Journal of Gender and Law* 12 (3): 421–429.

Claessens, Stijn, Erik Feijen, and Luc Laeven. 2008. "Political Connections and Preferential Access to Finance: The Role of Campaign Contributions." *Journal of Financial Economics* 88 (3): 554–580.

Clark, Mary L. 2002. "Changing the Face of the Law: How Women's Advocacy Groups Put Women on the Federal Judicial Appointments Agenda." *Yale Journal of Law and Feminism* 14 (2): 243–254.

———. 2011. "Carter's Groundbreaking Appointment of Women to the Federal Bench: His Other 'Human Rights' Record." *Journal of Gender, Social Policy and the Law* 11 (3): 1131–1163.

Clark, Roger E. 2006. "Forty Years of Judicial Merit Selection." *Colorado Lawyer* 35 (4): 4–5.

Clinton, William J. 1993. "Remarks Announcing the Nomination of Ruth Bader Ginsburg to Be a Supreme Court Associate Justice." *American Presidency Project*, June 14. Available at http://www.presidency.ucsb.edu/ws/?pid=46684.

Cole, Arthur Charles, ed. 1919. *Collections of the Illinois State Historical Society Library.* Vol. 14, *The Constitutional Debates of 1847.* Springfield: Illinois State Historical Library.

Collins, Todd, and Laura Moyer. 2008. "Gender, Race, and Intersectionality on the Federal Appellate Bench." *Political Research Quarterly* 61 (2): 219–227.

Committee for Economic Development. 2010. "Pennsylvania Statewide." May 25–26. Available at https://www.ced.org/pdf/papoll.pdf.

Conover, Milton. 1925. "Merit Systems of Civil Service in the States." *American Political Science Review* 19 (3): 544–560.

Cook, Beverly B. 1984. "Women Judges: A Preface to Their History." *Golden Gate University Law Review* 14 (3): 573–610.

Council of State Governments. 1960–2014. *The Book of the States.* Vols. 13–46. Lexington, KY: Council of State Governments.

Covington, Howard E., Jr., and Marion A. Ellis. 1999. *Terry Sanford: Politics, Progress, and Outrageous Ambitions.* Durham, NC: Duke University Press.

Craig v. Boren, 429 U.S. 190 (1976).

Crompton, J. Andrew. 2002. "Commentary: Pennsylvanian's Should Adopt a Merit Selection System for State Appellate Court Judges." *Dickinson Law Review* 106 (4): 755–768.

Davis, Angela J. 2007. *Arbitrary Justice: The Power of the American Prosecutor.* New York: Oxford University Press.

Davis, Richard. 2005. *Electing Justice: Fixing the Supreme Court Nomination Process.* New York: Oxford University Press.

Davis, Sue. 1986. "President Carter's Selection Reforms and Judicial Policymaking: A Voting Analysis of the United States Courts of Appeals." *American Politics Research* 14 (4): 328–344.

———. 1992. "Do Women Judges Speak 'in a Different Voice'? Carol Gilligan, Feminist Legal Theory, and the Ninth Circuit." *Wisconsin Women's Law Journal* 8 (1): 143–174.

Dempsey, Dave. 2006. *William G. Milliken: Michigan's Passionate Moderate.* Ann Arbor: University of Michigan Press.

Denning, Brannon P. 2012. "The Case against Appointing Politicians to the Supreme Court." *Florida Law Review* 64 (5): 31–33.

Dimino, Michael R. 2004. "The Futile Quest for a System of Judicial Merit Selection." *Albany Law Review* 67 (3): 803–820.

Dinan, John J. 2006. *The American State Constitutional Tradition.* Lawrence: University of Kansas Press.

Dodd, John L., Christopher Murray, Stephen B. Presser, Mark Pulliam, Alfred W. Putnam, and Paula M. Stannard. 2003. "The Case for Judicial Appointments." Judicial Appointments White Paper Task Force, January 1. Available at https://www.fed-soc.org/publications/detail/the-case-for-judicial-appointments.

Dodd, Walter F. 1923. "Illinois Rejects a New Constitution." *Minnesota Law Review* 7 (3): 177–186.

Dolan, Maura. 2014. "Expected California Supreme Court Nominee Leondra Kruger a 'Mind Blower.'" *Los Angeles Times,* November 24. Available at http://www.latimes.com/local/lanow/la-me-ln-leondra-kruger-state-supreme-court-20141124-story.html.

Douglass, Susan G. 1977. "Selection and Discipline of State Judges in Texas." *Houston Law Review* 14 (3): 672–699.

Dred Scott v. Sandford, 60 U.S. 393 (1857).

DuBois, Ellen Carol. 1978. *Feminism and Suffrage: The Emergence of an Independent Women's Movement in America, 1848–1969.* Ithaca: New York University Press.

Dubois, Philip L. 1983. "The Influence of Selection System and Region on the Characteristics of a Trial Court Bench: The Case of California." *Justice System Journal* 8 (1): 59–87.

———. 1984. "Voting Cues in Nonpartisan Trial Court Elections: A Multivariate Assessment." *Law and Society Review* 18 (3): 395–436.

———. 1990a. "The Politics of Innovation in State Courts: The Merit Plan of Judicial Selection." *Publius: The Journal of Federalism* 20 (1): 23–42.

———. 1990b. "Voter Responses to Court Reform: Merit Judicial Selection on the Ballot." *Judicature* 73 (5): 238–247.

Dunne, Gerald T. 1993. *The Missouri Supreme Court: From Dred Scott to Nancy Cruzan.* Columbia: University of Missouri Press.

Echaveste, Maria. 2002. "Brown to Black: The Politics of Judicial Appointments for Latinos." *Berkeley La Raza Law Journal* 13 (1): 39–42.

Emmert, Craig F., and Henry R. Glick. 1988. "The Selection of State Supreme Court Justices." *American Politics Quarterly* 16 (4): 445–465.

Epstein, Lee, and Jack Knight. 1997. *The Choices Justices Make.* Washington, DC: Congressional Quarterly Press.

Epstein, Lee, Jack Knight, and Andrew D. Martin. 2003. "The Norm of Prior Judicial Experience and Its Consequences for Career Diversity on the U.S. Supreme Court." *California Law Review* 91 (4): 903–955.

Epstein, Lee, Jack Knight, and Olga Shvetsova. 2001. "Comparing Judicial Selection Systems." *William and Mary Bill of Rights Journal* 10 (1): 7–36.

Epstein, Lee, William M. Landes, and Richard A. Posner. 2013. *The Behavior of Federal Judges: A Theoretical and Empirical Study of Rational Choice.* Cambridge, MA: Harvard University Press.

Epstein, Lee, Andrew D. Martin, Kevin M. Quinn, and Jeffrey A. Segal. 2009. "Circuit Effects: How the Norm of Federal Judicial Experience Biases the Supreme Court." *University of Pennsylvania Law Review* 157 (3): 833–880.

Epstein, Lee, Jeffrey A. Segal, Harold J. Spaeth, and Thomas G. Walker. 2012. *The Supreme Court Compendium: Data, Decisions, and Developments.* Washington, DC: Congressional Quarterly Press.

Epstein, Lee, Thomas G. Walker, Nancy Staudt, Scott Hendrickson, and Jason Roberts. 2013. *The U.S. Supreme Court Justices Database.* Available at http://epstein.wustl.edu/research/justicesdata.html.

Esterling, Kevin M., and Seth S. Andersen. 1999. "Diversity and the Judicial Merit Selection Process: A Statistical Report." Available at http://www.judicialselection.us/uploads/documents/Diversity_and_the_Judicial_Merit_Se_9C4863118945B.pdf.

Evans, Simon, and John Williams. 2008. "Appointing Australian Judges: A New Model." *Sydney Law Review* 30 (2): 295–328.

Faccio, Mara. 2006. "Politically Connected Firms." *American Economic Review* 96 (1): 369–386.

Faccio, Mara, Ronald W. Masulis, and John J. McConnell. 2006. "Political Connections and Corporate Bailouts." *Journal of Finance* 61 (6): 2597–2635.

Farber, Daniel A., and Suzanna Sherry. 2008. *Judgment Calls: Principle and Politics in Constitutional Law.* New York: Oxford University Press.

Farganis, Dion, and Justin Wedeking. 2011. "'No Hints, No Forecasts, No Previews': An Empirical Analysis of Supreme Court Nominee Candor from Harlan to Kagan." *Law and Society Review* 45 (3): 525–559.

Farhang, Sean, and Gregory Wawro. 2004. "Institutional Dynamics on the U.S. Court of Appeals: Minority Representation under Panel Decision Making." *Journal of Law, Economics, and Organization* 20 (2): 299–330.

Farrand, Max, ed. 1966. *The Records of the Federal Convention of 1987.* Vol. 2. New Haven, CT: Yale University Press.

Felice, John D., and John C. Kilwein. 1992. "Strike One, Strike Two . . . : The History of and Prospect for Judicial Reform in Ohio." *Judicature* 75 (4): 192–200.

Ferguson, Thomas, and Hans-Joachim Voth. 2008. "Betting on Hitler: The Value of Political Connections in Nazi Germany." *Quarterly Journal of Economics* 123 (1): 101–137.

Finley, Tillman J. 2003. "Judicial Selection in Alaska: Justifications and Proposed Courses of Reform." *Alaska Law Review* 20 (1): 49–77.

Fisch, Louise Ann. 1996. *All Rise: Reynaldo G. Garza, the First Mexican American Federal Judge.* College Station: Texas A&M Press.

Fisher, Harry M. 1937. "The Selection of Judges for Cook County: The Chicago Bar Association Plan." *Illinois Law Review* 31 (7): 898–904.

Fisman, Raymond. 2001. "Estimating the Value of Political Connections." *American Economic Review* 91 (4): 1095–1102.

Fisman, Raymond, and Yongxiang Wang. 2015. "The Mortality Cost of Political Connections." *Review of Economic Studies* 82 (2): 1346–1382.

Fitzpatrick, Brian T. 2008. "Election as Appointment: The Tennessee Plan Reconsidered." *Tennessee Law Review* 75 (3): 473–500.

———. 2009. "The Politics of Merit Selection." *Missouri Law Review* 74 (3): 675–709.

Fournet, Monique Renee, Kyle C. Kopko, Dana Whitmer, and Lawrence Baum. 2009. "Evolution of Judicial Careers in the Federal Courts, 1789–2008." *Judicature* 93 (2): 62–74.

Frederick, Brian, and Matthew J. Streb. 2008. "Paying the Price for a Seat on the Bench: Campaign Spending in Contested State Intermediate Appellate Court Elections." *State Politics and Policy Quarterly* 8 (4): 410–429.

Fridkin, Kim L., and Patrick J. Kenney. 2014. "How the Gender of U.S. Senators Influences People's Understanding and Engagement in Politics." *Journal of Politics* 76 (4): 1017–1031.

Friedman, Barry. 2009. *The Will of the People: How Public Opinion Has Influenced the Supreme Court and Shaped the Meaning of the Constitution*. New York: Farrar, Straus, and Giroux.

Friedman, Jane M. 1993. *America's First Woman Lawyer: The Biography of Myra Bradwell*. Amherst, MA: Prometheus Books.

Frontiero v. Richardson, 411 U.S. 677 (1973).

Fund for Modern Courts. n.d. "Why Merit Selection?" Available at http://moderncourts.org/advocacy/judicial-selection/why-merit-selection (accessed October 14, 2015).

Gailmard, Sean, and John W. Patty. 2013. *Learning while Governing: Expertise and Accountability in the Executive Branch*. Chicago: University of Chicago Press.

Gardner, Henry A., Harry M. Fisher, and Edward M. Martin. 1936–1937. "The Selection of Judges for Cook County: The Chicago Bar Association Plan." *Illinois Law Review* 31 (7): 893–898.

Garrison, Chad. 2007. "The Mystery of Lloyd Gaines." *Riverfront Times*, April 4. Available at http://www.riverfronttimes.com/stlouis/the-mystery-of-lloyd-gaines/Content?oid=2479115.

Gauch, James E. 1989. "The Intended Role of the Senate in Supreme Court Appointments." *University of Chicago Law Review* 56 (1): 337–366.

Gay, Claudine. 2002. "Spirals of Trust? The Effect of Descriptive Representation on the Relationship between Citizens and Their Government." *American Journal of Political Science* 46 (4): 717–732.

George, Tracey E. 2001. "Court Fixing." *Arizona Law Review* 43 (1): 9–62.

Geyh, Charles Gardner. 2008. "The Endless Judicial Selection Debate and Why It Matters for Judicial Independence." *Georgetown Journal of Legal Ethics* 21 (4): 1259–1282.

———, ed. 2011. *What's Law Got to Do with It? What Judges Do, Why They Do It, and What's at Stake.* Stanford, CA: Stanford University Press.

———. 2015. "The Jekyll and Hyde of First Amendment Limits on the Regulation of Judicial Campaign Speech." *Vanderbilt Law Review En Banc* 68:83–97.

Gibson, James L. 2012. *Electing Judges: The Surprising Effects of Campaigning on Judicial Legitimacy.* Chicago: University of Chicago Press.

Gibson, James L., and Gregory A. Caldeira. 2012. "Campaign Support, Conflicts of Interest, and Judicial Impartiality: Can Recusals Rescue the Legitimacy of Courts?" *Journal of Politics* 74 (1): 18–34.

———. 2013. "Judicial Impartiality, Campaign Contributions, and Recusals: Results from a National Survey." *Journal of Empirical Legal Studies* 10 (1): 76–103.

Gill, Michael Z., and Andrew B. Hall. 2015. "How Judicial Identity Changes the Text of Legal Rulings." *Social Science Research Network*, June 19. Available at http://papers.ssrn.com/sol3/papers.cfm?abstract_id=2620781.

Ginsburg, Ruth Bader. 1973. "The Need for the Equal Rights Amendment." *American Bar Association Journal* 59 (9): 1013–1019.

———. 1978. "The Equal Rights Amendment Is the Way." *Harvard Women's Law Journal* 1 (1): 19–26.

———. 2004. "Remarks on Women's Progress at the Bar and on the Bench." *Cornell Law Review* 89 (4): 801–807.

Ginsburg, Ruth Bader, and Laura W. Brill. 1995. "Women in the Federal Judiciary: Three Way Pavers and the Exhilarating Change President Carter Wrought." *Fordham Law Review* 64 (2): 281–290.

Glick, Henry R. 1978. "The Promise and the Performance of the Missouri Plan: Judicial Selection in the Fifty States." *University of Miami Law Review* 32 (3): 509–542.

Glick, Henry R., and Craig F. Emmert. 1987. "Selection Systems and Judicial Characteristics: The Recruitment of State Supreme Court Judges." *Judicature* 70 (4): 228–235.

Goelzhauser, Greg. 2011. "Diversifying State Supreme Courts." *Law and Society Review* 45 (3): 761–781.

———. 2012. "Accountability and Judicial Performance: Evidence from Case Dispositions." *Justice System Journal* 33 (3): 249–261.

———. 2013. "Prosecutorial Discretion under Resource Constraints: Budget Allocations and Local Death-Charging Decisions." *Judicature* 96 (4): 161–168.

Goelzhauser, Greg, and Damon M. Cann. 2014. "Judicial Independence and Opinion Clarity on State Supreme Courts." *State Politics and Policy Quarterly* 14 (2): 123–141.

Goesaert v. Cleary, 335 U.S. 464 (1948).

Gofen, Charlie. 1987. "Lawyer Group Opposes Merit Judge Selection." *Chicago Tribune*, December 11, p. 22.

Goldman, Sheldon. 1978. "A Profile of Carter's Judicial Nominees." *Judicature* 62 (5): 246–254.

———. 1989. "Reagan's Judicial Legacy: Completing the Puzzle and Summing Up." *Judicature* 72 (6): 313–330.

———. 1997. *Picking Federal Judges: Lower Court Selection from Roosevelt through Reagan*. New Haven, CT: Yale University Press.

Goldschmidt, Jona. 1994. "Merit Selection: Current Status, Procedures, and Issues." *University of Miami Law Review* 49 (1): 1–126.

Goldstein, Adam. 2007. "Judicial Selection as It Relates to Gender Equality on the Bench." *Cardozo Journal of Law and Gender* 13 (2): 369–406.

Gordon, Sanford C., and Gregory A. Huber. 2002. "Citizen Oversight and the Electoral Incentives of Criminal Prosecutors." *American Journal of Political Science* 46 (2): 334–351.

"Governor Lingle Names Rom Trader as First Circuit Court Judge." 2009. Available at http://archive.lingle.hawaii.gov/govgallery/news/releases/2008/governor-lingle-names-rom-trader-as-first-circuit.

"Governor Rendell Endorses Judicial Merit Selection Reform Bill." 2009. PR Newswire, December 7. Available at http://www.prnewswire.com/news-releases/governor-rendell-endorses-judicial-merit-selection-reform-bill-78714097.html.

Graczyk, Michael. 2010. "Judge Sharon Keller Speaks Out after Reprimand Tossed." *Dallas Morning News*, October 20. Available at http://www.dallasnews.com/news/state/headlines/20101020-Judge-Sharon-Keller-speaks-out-after-7068.ece.

Graham, Barbara Luck. 1990. "Do Judicial Selection Systems Matter? A Study of Black Representation on State Courts." *American Politics Quarterly* 18 (3): 316–336.

Granfield, Robert, and Lynn Mather, eds. 2009. *Private Lawyers and the Public Interest: The Evolving Role of Pro Bono in the Legal Profession*. New York: Oxford University Press.

Greenburg, Jan Crawford. 2007. *Supreme Conflict: The Inside Story of the Struggle for Control of the United States Supreme Court*. New York: Penguin.

Gryski, Gerard S., Eleanor C. Main, and William J. Dixon. 1986. "Models of State High Court Decision Making in Sex Discrimination Cases." *Journal of Politics* 48 (1): 143–155.

Hagopian, Frances. 1994. "Traditional Politics against State Transformation in Brazil." In *State Power and Social Forces: Domination and Transformation in the Third World*, edited by Joel S. Migdal, Atul Kohli, and Vivienne Shue, 37–64. Cambridge: Cambridge University Press.

Haider-Markel, Don. 2010. *Out and Running: Gay and Lesbian Candidates, Elections, and Policy Representation*. Washington, DC: Georgetown University Press.

Haire, Susan Brodie. 2001. "Rating the Ratings of the American Bar Association Standing Committee on Federal Judiciary." *Justice System Journal* 22 (1): 1–17.

Hall, Hewlett A. 1909. "Symposium: What Is the Best Method for Selecting Judges and Solicitors-General?" In *Report of the Twenty-Sixth Annual Session of the Georgia Bar Association*, edited by Orville A. Park, 222–229. Atlanta, GA: Chas. P. Byrd.

Hall, Kermit L. 1976a. "101 Men: The Social Composition and Recruitment of the Antebellum Lower Federal Judiciary, 1829–1861." *Rutgers-Camden Law Journal* 7 (2): 199–227.

———. 1976b. "240 Men: The Antebellum Lower Federal Judiciary, 1829–1861." *Vanderbilt Law Review* 29 (5): 1089–1130.

———. 1976c. "Social Backgrounds and Judicial Recruitment: A Nineteenth-Century Perspective on the Lower Federal Judiciary." *Western Political Quarterly* 29 (2): 243–257.

———. 1983. "The Judiciary on Trial: State Constitutional Reform and the Rise of an Elected Judiciary, 1846–1860." *Historian* 45 (3): 337–354.

———. 1984. "Progressive Reform and the Decline of Democratic Accountability: The Popular Election of State Supreme Court Judges, 1850–1920." *American Bar Foundation Research Journal* 9 (2): 345–369.

———. 1989. *The Magic Mirror: Law in American History*. New York: Oxford University Press.

Hall, Matthew E. K., and Jason Harold Windett. 2013. "New Data on State Supreme Court Cases." *State Politics and Policy Quarterly* 13 (4): 427–445.

Hall, Melinda Gann. 1985. "Docket Control as an Influence on Judicial Voting." *Justice System Journal* 10 (2): 243–255.

———. 1987. "Constituent Influence in State Supreme Courts: Conceptual Notes and a Case Study." *Journal of Politics* 49 (4): 1117–1124.

———. 1992. "Electoral Politics and Strategic Voting in State Supreme Courts." *Journal of Politics* 54 (2): 427–446.

———. 2001a. "State Supreme Courts in American Democracy: Probing the Myths of Judicial Reform." *American Political Science Review* 95 (2): 315–330.

———. 2001b. "Voluntary Retirements from State Supreme Courts: Assessing Democratic Pressures to Relinquish the Bench." *Journal of Politics* 63 (4): 1112–1140.

———. 2007. "Voting in State Supreme Court Elections: Competition and Context as Democratic Incentives." *Journal of Politics* 69 (4): 1147–1159.

———. 2013. "Representation in State Supreme Courts: Evidence from the Terminal Term." *Political Research Quarterly* 67 (2): 335–346.

———. 2015. *Attacking Judges: How Campaign Advertising Influences State Supreme Court Elections*. Stanford, CA: Stanford University Press.

Hall, Melinda Gann, and Chris W. Bonneau. 2006. "Does Quality Matter? Challengers in State Supreme Court Elections." *American Journal of Political Science* 50 (1): 20–33.

———. 2008. "Mobilizing Interest: The Effects of Money on Citizen Participation in State Supreme Court Elections." *American Journal of Political Science* 52 (3): 457–470.

———. 2013. "Attack Advertising, the *White* Decision, and Voter Participation in State Supreme Court Elections." *Political Research Quarterly* 66 (1): 115–126.

Hall, Melinda Gann, and Paul R. Brace. 1992. "Toward an Integrated Model of Judicial Voting Behavior." *American Politics Research* 20 (2): 147–168.

———. 1996. "Justices' Responses to Case Facts: An Interactive Model." *American Politics Research* 24 (2): 237–261.

Hall, Michael. 2009. "The Judgment of Sharon Keller." *Texas Monthly*, August. Available at http://www.texasmonthly.com/story/judgment-sharon-keller/page/0/2.

Hamilton, Alexander. 1788. "Federalist No. 76: The Appointing Power of the Executive." In *The Federalist*, by Alexander Hamilton, James Madison, and John Jay. New York: J. and A. McLean. Available at http://avalon.law.yale.edu/18th_century/fed76.asp.

Hancock, Peter. 2015. "Kansas Judiciary Shows Little Racial Diversity." *Lawrence Journal-World*, February 7. Available at http://www2.ljworld.com/news/2015/feb/07/kansas-judiciary-shows-little-racial-diversity.

Handler, Joel F., Ellen Jane Hollingsworth, Howard E. Erlanger, and Jack Ladinsky. 1975. "The Public Interest Activities of Private Practice Lawyers." *American Bar Association Journal* 61 (11): 1388–1398.

Hanssen, F. Andrew. 2004. "Learning about Judicial Independence: Institutional Change in the State Courts." *Journal of Legal Studies* 33 (2): 431–473.

Hardin, Peter. 2011. "NC Governor Creates Judicial Screening Commission." *Gavel Grab*, April 6. Available at http://gavelgrab.org/?p=19537.

Hargrove, Monica R. 2010. "Evolution of Black Lawyers in Corporate America: From the Road Less Traveled to Managing the Major Highways." *Howard Law Journal* 53 (3): 749–800.

Hasday, Jill Elaine. 2000. "Contest and Consent: A Legal History of Marital Rape." *California Law Review* 88 (5): 1373–1505.

Headlam, Cecil, ed. 1908. *Calendar of State Papers, Colonial Series, America and West Indies*. London: Wyman and Sons.

Heilman, Dan. 2008. "Are Asian Americans Underrepresented on Minnesota's Bench?" *Minnesota Lawyer*, August 11. Available at http://minnlawyer.com/2008/08/11/are-asian-americans-underrepresented-on-minnesota8217s-bench063.

Henderson, William D. 2013. "Successful Lawyer Skills and Behaviors." In *Essential Qualities of the Professional Lawyer*, edited by Paul A. Haskins, 53–68. Chicago: American Bar Association.

Hermens, F. A. 1940. "Exit the Boss." *Review of Politics* 2 (4): 385–404.

Hillman, Amy J. 2005. "Politicians on the Board of Directors: Do Connections Affect the Bottom Line?" *Journal of Management* 31 (3): 464–481.

Hinkle, Rachael K., Andrew D. Martin, Jonathan David Shaub, and Emerson H. Tiller. 2012. "A Positive Theory and Empirical Analysis of Strategic Word Choice in District Court Opinions." *Journal of Legal Analysis* 4 (2): 407–444.

Holmes, Lisa M. 2012. "The Composition of the Federal Bench: Nominating and Confirming Judges from the Private Sector." *Social Science Research Network*, September 16. Available at http://papers.ssrn.com/sol3/papers.cfm?abstract_id=2107437.

Holmes, Lisa M., and Jolly A. Emrey. 2006. "Court Diversification: Staffing the State Courts of Last Resort through Interim Appointments." *Justice System Journal* 27 (1): 1–13.

Horwitz, Morton J. 1975. "The Rise of Legal Formalism." *American Journal of Legal History* 19 (4): 251–264.

Hosmer, James K. 1896. *The Life of Thomas Hutchinson: Royal Governor of the Province of Massachusetts Bay.* Boston: Houghton, Mifflin.

Howard, Robert M., and Amy Steigerwalt. 2012. *Judging Law and Policy: Courts and Policymaking in the American Political System.* New York: Routledge.

Hsu, Josh. 2006. "Asian American Judges: Identity, Their Narratives, and Diversity on the Bench." *Asian Pacific American Law Journal* 11 (1): 92–119.

Huber, Gregory A., and Sanford C. Gordon. 2004. "Accountability and Coercion: Is Justice Blind When It Runs for Office." *American Journal of Political Science* 48 (2): 247–263.

Hurst, James Willard. 1950. *The Growth of American Law: The Law Makers.* Boston: Little, Brown.

Hurwitz, Mark S. 2010. "Selection System, Diversity and the Michigan Supreme Court." *Wayne Law Review* 56 (2): 691–704.

Hurwitz, Mark S., and Drew Noble Lanier. 2001. "Women and Minorities on State and Federal Appellate Benches, 1985 and 1999." *Judicature* 85 (2): 84–92.

———. 2003. "Explaining Judicial Diversity: The Differential Ability of Women and Minorities to Attain Seats on State Supreme and Appellate Courts." *State Politics and Policy Quarterly* 3 (4): 329–352.

———. 2008. "Diversity in State and Federal Appellate Courts: Change and Continuity across 20 Years." *Justice System Journal* 29 (1): 47–70.

In re Goodell, 39 Wis. 232 (1875).

In re Goodell, 48 Wis. 693 (1879).

"Introductory Comments—Governor Sam Brownback." n.d. Available at https://governor.ks.gov/docs/default-source/documents/court-of-appeals-nominee-announcement-text.pdf?sfvrsn=4 (accessed October 14, 2015).

Jackson, Jeffrey D. 2000. "The Selection of Judges in Kansas: A Comparison of Systems." *Journal of the Kansas Bar Association* 69 (1): 32–42.

Jacob, Herbert. 1964. "The Effect of Institutional Differences in the Recruitment Process: The Case of State Judges." *Journal of Public Law* 13 (1): 104–119.

Jenks, Barton P., III. 1996. "Rhode Island's New Judicial Merit Selection Law." *Roger Williams University Law Review* 1 (1): 63–86.

Journal of the Constitutional Convention 1920–1922 of the State of Illinois. 1922. Springfield: Illinois State Journal.

Kales, Albert M. 1914a. "Methods of Selecting and Retiring Judges." *Journal of the American Judicature Society* 6:29–52.

———. 1914b. *Unpopular Government in the United States.* Chicago: University of Chicago Press.

Kang, Michael S., and Joanna M. Shepherd. 2013. "The Partisan Foundations of Judicial Campaign Finance." *Southern California Law Review* 86 (6): 1239–1308.

Kanowitz, Leo. 1968. "Sex-Based Discrimination in American Law III: Title VII of the 1964 Civil Rights Act and the Equal Pay Act of 1963." *Hastings Law Journal* 20 (1): 305–360.

Karin, Marcy Lynn. 2004. "Esther Morris and Her Equality State: From Council Bill 70 to Life on the Bench." *American Journal of Legal History* 46 (3): 300–343.

Kastellec, Jonathan P. 2013. "Racial Diversity and Judicial Influence on Appellate Courts." *American Journal of Political Science* 57 (1): 167–183.

Katz, Matt. 2013. "'Diversity' and Its Definition at Issue in Christie's Picks for High Court." *Philadelphia Inquirer,* January 2, p. A01.

"Keep Courts on Track; Take Judges off Ballot." 1996. *Palm Beach Post,* March 16, p. 14A.

Kenney, Sally J. 2013. *Gender and Justice: Why Women in the Judiciary Really Matter.* New York: Routledge.

Kirkendall, Richard S. 1986. *A History of Missouri.* Vol. 5. Columbia: University of Missouri Press.

Klarman, Michael J. 2004. *From Jim Crow to Civil Rights: The Supreme Court and the Struggle for Racial Equality.* New York: Oxford University Press.

Klein, David, and Lawrence Baum. 2001. "Ballot Information and Voting Decisions in Judicial Elections." *Political Research Quarterly* 54 (4): 709–728.

Klemme, Chris. 2002. "Jacksonian Justice: The Evolution of the Elective Judiciary in Texas, 1836–1850." *Southwestern Historical Quarterly* 105 (3): 428–450.

Korobkin, Russell. 1998. "In Praise of Law School Rankings: Solutions to Coordination and Collective Action Problems." *Texas Law Review* 77 (2): 403–428.

Krajelis, Bethany. 2012. "Debate over Merit Selection Continues; Recusal, Public Financing Proposals Pushed in Meantime." *Madison County Record,* September 27. Available at http://madisonrecord.com/stories/510574051 -debate-over-merit-selection-continues-recusal-public-financing-proposals -pushed-in-meantime.

Krasno, Jonathan S., and Donald Phillip Green. 1988. "Preempting Quality Challengers in House Elections." *Journal of Politics* 50 (4): 920–936.

Kritzer, Herbert M. 2015. *Justices on the Ballot: Continuity and Change in State Supreme Court Elections.* New York: Cambridge University Press.

Kritzer, Herbert M., Paul Brace, Melinda Gann Hall, and Brent T. Boyea. 2007. "The Business of State Supreme Courts, Revisited." *Journal of Empirical Legal Studies* 4 (2): 427–439.

Krivosha, Norman. 1987. "Acquiring Judges by the Merit Selection Method: The Case for Adopting Such a Method." *Southwestern Law Journal* 40 (6): 15–22.

———. 1990. "In Celebration of the 50th Anniversary of Merit Selection." *Judicature* 74 (3): 128–132.

Kruse, Becky. 2001. "Luck and Politics: Judicial Selection Methods and Their Effect on Women on the Bench." *Wisconsin Women's Law Journal* 16 (1): 67–86.

Langer, Laura. 2002. *Judicial Review in State Supreme Courts*. Albany: State University of New York Press.

Langston, John Mercer. 1894. *From the Virginia Plantation to the National Capitol; Or, the First and Only Negro Representative in Congress from the Old Dominion*. Hartford, CT: American.

Lanier, Drew Noble, and Roger Handberg. 2011. "Diversity and Merit Selection: The Impact of Judicial Nominating Commissions on the Gender Demographics of Florida's Appellate Judges." *Social Science Research Network*, May 20. Available at http://papers.ssrn.com/sol3/papers.cfm?abstract_id=1847809.

Larsen, Lawrence H., and Nancy J. Hulston. 1997. *Pendergast!* Columbia: University of Missouri Press.

Laski, Harold J. 1926. "The Technique of Judicial Appointment." *Michigan Law Review* 24 (6): 529–543.

Lawrence, Susan E. 1990. *The Poor in Court: The Legal Services Program and Supreme Court Decision Making*. Princeton, NJ: Princeton University Press.

League of Women Voters of Hawaii. 2003. "Merit Selection of Judges and Justices." Available at http://www.lwv-hawaii.com/pos_merit.htm.

League of Women Voters of Illinois. 2014. *Where We Stand: 2013–2015 Program*. Chicago: League of Women Voters of Illinois. Available at http://www.weebly.com/uploads/1/5/9/8/15985276/where_we_stand_2013-2015_web.pdf#page=15.

Lerner, Renée Lettow. 2007. "From Popular Control to Independence: Reform of the Elected Judiciary in Boss Tweed's New York." *George Mason Law Review* 15 (1): 109–160.

Little, Laura E. 2001. "The ABA's Role in Prescreening Federal Judicial Candidates: Are We Ready to Give Up on the Lawyers?" *William and Mary Bill of Rights Journal* 10 (1): 37–73.

Long, Alex B. 2002. "An Historical Perspective on Judicial Selection Methods in Virginia and West Virginia." *Journal of Law and Politics* 18 (3): 691–772.

Long, J. Scott, and Jeremy Freese. 2006. *Regression Models for Categorical Dependent Variables Using Stata*. 2nd ed. College Station, TX: Stata Press.

Louisiana Bar Association. 1920. *Report of the Special Committee on Judiciary Ordinances of the New Constitution*. New Orleans, LA: E. P. Andree.

Lowe, Stanley R. 1971. "Voluntary Merit Selection." *Judicature* 55 (4): 161–168.

Lowry, Bryan. 2014a. "Brownback Says Stegall Has No Inside Track to Be on Kansas Supreme Court." *Wichita Eagle*, August 15. Available at http://www.kansas.com/news/politics-government/article1234832.html.

———. 2014b. "Gov. Sam Brownback Names Former Aide Caleb Stegall to Supreme Court." *Wichita Eagle*, August 29. Available at http://www.kansas.com/news/politics-government/article1323768.html.

Lupton, John A. 2011. "Myra Bradwell and the Profession of Law: Case Documents." *Journal of Supreme Court History* 36 (3): 236–263.

Mah, John K. C. 1994. "Diversity of Bench Takes the Stand in Simpson Case." *Los Angeles Times*, August 8. Available at http://articles.latimes.com/1994-08-08/local/me-24768_1_minority-judges.

Maltzman, Forrest, James F. Spriggs, and Paul J. Wahlbeck. 2000. *Crafting Law on the Supreme Court: The Collegial Game*. New York: Cambridge University Press.

Mansbridge, Jane J. 1986. *Why We Lost the ERA*. Chicago: University of Chicago Press.

———. 1999. "Should Blacks Represent Blacks and Women Represent Women? A Contingent 'Yes.'" *Journal of Politics* 61 (3): 628–657.

Martin, Elaine. 1987. "Gender and Judicial Selection: A Comparison of the Reagan and Carter Administration." *Judicature* 71 (3): 136–142.

———. 1990. "Men and Women on the Bench: Vive la Difference." *Judicature* 73 (4): 204–208.

Martin, Elaine, and Barry Pyle. 2002. "Gender and Racial Diversification of State Supreme Courts." *Women and Politics* 24 (2): 35–52.

———. 2005. "State High Courts and Divorce: The Impact of Judicial Gender." *University of Toledo Law Review* 36 (4): 923–948.

Maute, Judith L. 2000. "Selecting Justice in State Courts: The Ballot Box or the Backroom." *South Texas Law Review* 41 (4): 1197–1246.

———. 2007. "English Reforms to Judicial Selection: Comparative Lessons for American States." *Fordham Urban Law Journal* 34 (1): 387–424.

Maveety, Nancy. 1996. *Justice Sandra Day O'Connor: Strategist on the Supreme Court*. Boston: Rowman and Littlefield.

McCormick, Charles T. 1935. "Judicial Selection—Current Plans and Trends." *Illinois Law Review* 30 (4): 446–468.

McCrory, Pat. 2013. Executive Order No. 1. Available at http://governor.nc.gov/document/eo-1-establishing-procedure-appointment-justices-and-judges.

McLaurin v. Oklahoma State Regents for Higher Education, 339 U.S. 637 (1950).

McLeod, Aman. 2012. "The Party on the Bench: Partisanship, Judicial Selection Commissions, and State High-Court Appointments." *Justice System Journal* 33 (3): 262–274.

Mikva, Abner J. 1982. "Judicial Selection: Casting a Wider Net." *Annals of the American Academy of Political and Social Science* 462:125–135.

Miller, Banks, and Brett Curry. 2013. "The Effect of *Per Se* Recusal Rules on Donor Behavior in Judicial Elections." *Justice System Journal* 34 (2): 125–151.

Miranda v. Arizona, 384 U.S. 436 (1966).

Missouri ex rel. Gaines v. Canada, 305 U.S. 337 (1938).

Montini, E. J. 2005. "Rehnquist Is No. 1, O'Connor Is No. 3, Baloney Is No. 2." *Arizona Republic*, July 12. Available at http://www.azcentral.com/news/columns/articles/0712montini12.html?&wired.

Moran, Tom. 2012. "Diversity Is Good, but Gov. Chris Christie's Judge Picks Are Mediocre." *NJ.com*, January 29. Available at http://blog.nj.com/njv_tom_moran/2012/01/diversity_is_good_but_gov_chri.html.

Morris, Frank. 2014. "The New Justice in Kansas: Judicial Selection and the Governor's Race." *KCUR*, September 12. Available at http://kcur.org/post/new-justice-kansas-judicial-selection-and-governor-s-race.

Mott, Rodney L., Spencer D. Albright, and Helen R. Semmerling. 1933. "Judicial Personnel." *Annals of the American Academy of Political and Social Science* 167:143–155.

Murphy, Jan. 2013. "Four Former Governors Team Up to Push Judicial Merit Selection." *PennLive*, March 18. Available at http://www.pennlive.com/midstate/index.ssf/2013/03/four_former_governors_team_up.html.

Myers, Gustavaus. 1917. *The History of Tammany Hall*. 2nd ed. New York: Boni and Liveright.

Myers, K. O. 2013. "Merit Selection and Diversity on the Bench." *Indiana Law Review* 46 (1): 43–58.

Myers, Linda. 2007. "Distinguished Jurist in the Best Sense: Three Days with Justice Sandra Day O'Connor." *Cornell Law Forum* 34 (1): 4–7.

Nelson, Caleb. 1993. "A Re-evaluation of Scholarly Explanations for the Rise of the Elective Judiciary in Antebellum America." *American Journal of Legal History* 37 (2): 190–224.

Nelson, Michael J. 2013. "Elections and Explanations: Judicial Retention and the Readability of Judicial Opinions." Working paper, September 9. Available at http://mjnelson.org/papers/NelsonReadabilityAugust2013.pdf.

———. 2014. "Duel(ing) Constitutions: State Constitutions and Judicial Federalism." Working paper, February 21. Available at http://capr.la.psu.edu/documents/NelsonJudFedFeb21.pdf.

Newman, Sandra Schultz, and Daniel Mark Isaacs. 2004. "Historical Overview of the Judicial Selection Process in the United States: Is the Electoral System in Pennsylvania Unjustified?" *Villanova Law Review* 49 (1): 1–54.

New Mexico Supreme Court. 2010. "Supreme Court Justices of the State of New Mexico since Statehood." Available at https://nmsupremecourt.nmcourts.gov/justices/justices_since_statehood.pdf.

Norgren, Jill. 2013. *Rebels at the Bar: The Fascinating, Forgotten Stories of America's First Women Lawyers*. New York: New York University Press.

Norris, John T. 1909. "Symposium: What Is the Best Method for Selecting Judges and Solicitors-General?" In *Report of the Twenty-Sixth Annual Session of the Georgia Bar Association*, edited by Orville A. Park, 215–219. Atlanta, GA: Chas. P. Byrd.

O'Connor, Sandra Day. 1996. "The History of the Women's Suffrage Movement." *Vanderbilt Law Review* 49 (3): 657–676.

———. 2001. "Courthouse Dedication: Justice O'Connor Reflects on Arizona's Judiciary." *Arizona Law Review* 43 (1): 1–8.

———. 2009. "The Essentials and Expendables of the Missouri Plan." *Missouri Law Review* 74 (3): 479–494.

———. 2014. "The O'Connor Judicial Selection Plan." Available at http://iaals .du.edu/images/wygwam/documents/publications/OConnor_Plan.pdf.

Official Report of the Debates and Proceedings, in the State Convention, Assembled May 5th, 1853, to Revise and Amend the Constitution of the Commonwealth of Massachusetts. 1853. Vol. 1. Boston: White and Potter.

Ogletree, Charles J., Jr. 1993. "Beyond Justifications: Seeking Motivations to Sustain Public Defenders." *Harvard Law Review* 106 (6): 1239–1294.

Olmstead, Rob. 2009. "Few Hispanics Found on Bench Locally." *Chicago Daily Herald*, May 27, p. 11.

Olszewski, Peter Paul, Sr. 2004. "Who's Judging Whom? Why Popular Elections Are Preferable to Merit Selection Systems." *Penn State Law Review* 109 (1): 1–16.

O'Neil, Timothy P. 2007. "'The Stepford Justices': The Need for Experiential Diversity on the Roberts Court." *Oklahoma Law Review* 69 (4): 701–736.

Ovtchinnikov, Alexei V., and Eva Pantaleoni. 2012. "Individual Political Contributions and Firm Performance." *Journal of Financial Economics* 105 (2): 367–392.

Owens, Annie L. 2005. "'All Politics Is Local': The Politics of Merit-Based Federal Judicial Selection in Wisconsin." *Marquette Law Review* 88 (5): 1031–1053.

Owens, George W. 1909. "Symposium: What Is the Best Method for Selecting Judges and Solicitors-General?" In *Report of the Twenty-Sixth Annual Session of the Georgia Bar Association*, edited by Orville A. Park, 208–215. Atlanta, GA: Chas. P. Byrd.

Owens, Ryan J., Alexander Tahk, Patrick C. Wohlfarth, and Amanda C. Bryan. 2015. "Nominating Commissions, Judicial Retention, and Forward-Looking Behavior on State Supreme Courts: An Empirical Examination of Selection and Retention Methods." *State Politics and Policy Quarterly* 15 (2): 211–238.

Padilla, Fernando V. 1974. "Socialization of Chicano Judges and Attorneys." *Aztian: A Journal of Chicano Studies* 5 (1–2): 261–294.

Peppers, Todd C. 2006. *Courtiers of the Marble Palace: The Rise and Influence of the Supreme Court Law Clerk.* Stanford, CA: Stanford University Press.

———. 2007. "Birth of an Institution: Horace Gray and the Lost Law Clerks." *Journal of Supreme Court History* 33 (3): 229–248.

Peppers, Todd C., Michael W. Giles, and Bridget Tainer-Parkins. 2008. "Inside Judicial Chambers: How Federal District Court Judges Select and Use Their Law Clerks." *Albany Law Review* 71 (2): 623–646.

Peppers, Todd C., and Artemus Ward, eds. 2012. *In Chambers: Stories of Supreme Court Law Clerks and Their Justices.* Charlottesville: University of Virginia Press.

Perdue, Beverly Eaves. 2012. Executive Order No. 37. Available at http://digital
.ncdcr.gov/cdm/ref/collection/p16062coll5/id/20047.

Peretti, Terri L. 2007. "Where Have All the Politicians Gone? Recruiting for the
Modern Supreme Court." *Judicature* 91 (3): 112–122.

Petrie, Bruce I. 1974. Remarks to the Ohio Constitutional Revision Commission.
In *Ohio Constitutional Revision Commission, 1970–1977: Proceedings Research*,
vol. 8, 3850–3855. Columbus: Ohio Constitutional Revision Commission.
Available at http://www.lsc.ohio.gov/ocrc/v8%20pgs%203850-4328%20
judiciary%204329-4394%20education-bill%20of%20rights.pdf.

Phenicie, Mark E. 2012. "Written Testimony before the House Judiciary Committee: Appointment of Appellate Judges." March 1. Available at http://www
.legis.state.pa.us/cfdocs/legis/TR/transcripts/2012_0023_0016_TSTMNY
.pdf.

Phillips, Thomas R. 2009. "The Merits of Merit Selection." *Harvard Journal of
Law and Public Policy* 32 (1): 67–96.

Pitkin, Hanna Fenichel. 1967. *The Concept of Representation*. Berkeley: University
of California Press.

Plessy v. Ferguson, 163 U.S. 537 (1896).

Pope, John D. 1909. "Symposium: What Is the Best Method for Selecting Judges
and Solicitors-General?" In *Report of the Twenty-Sixth Annual Session of the
Georgia Bar Association*, edited by Orville A. Park, 219–222. Atlanta, GA:
Chas. P. Byrd.

Posner, Richard A. 1999. *The Federal Courts: Challenge and Reform*. Cambridge,
MA: Harvard University Press.

———. 2005. "A Political Court." *Harvard Law Review* 119 (1): 32–102.

———. 2010. "Some Realism about Judges: A Reply to Edwards and Livermore."
Duke Law Journal 59 (6): 1177–1186.

Pound, Roscoe. 1906. "The Causes of Popular Dissatisfaction with the Administration of Justice." *American Lawyer* 14 (10): 445–451.

———. 1908. "Mechanical Jurisprudence." *Columbia Law Review* 8 (8): 605–623.

Primus, Richard A. 2004. "Bolling Alone." *Columbia Law Review* 104 (4):
975–1041.

Proceedings and Debates of the Constitutional Convention of the State of Ohio. 1912.
Vol. 1. Columbus, OH: F. J. Heer.

"Proceedings of the Fifty-Fourth Annual Meeting." 1953. *Nebraska Law Review*
33:141–381.

Provine, Doris Marie. 1986. *Judging Credentials: Nonlawyer Judges and the Politics
of Professionalism*. Chicago: University of Chicago Press.

Puro, Marsha, Peter J. Bergerson, and Steven Puro. 1985. "An Analysis of Judicial
Diffusion: Adoption of the Missouri Plan in the American States." *Publius:
The Journal of Federalism* 15 (4): 85–97.

Quinn, William F. 1960. "Judicial Administration and Selection: Old Problems in
Our Newest State." *Journal of the American Judicature Society* 44 (5): 86–92.

Rajagopal, Krishnadas. 2015. "Collegium System to Continue until NJAC Is in Place." *The Hindu*, February 7. Available at http://www.thehindu.com/news/national/collegium-system-to-continue-until-njac-is-in-place/article6866754.ece.

Ramsey, Ross. 2012. "Make It One More Supreme Court Justice from the Perry Camp." *New York Times*, December 1. Available at http://www.nytimes.com/2012/12/02/us/jeffrey-boyd-is-7th-perry-appointee-on-texas-high-court.html.

Reddick, Malia. 2002. "Merit Selection: A Review of the Social Scientific Literature." *Dickinson Law Review* 106 (4): 729–746.

Reddick, Malia, Michael J. Nelson, and Rachel Paine Caufield. 2009. "Racial and Gender Diversity on State Courts." *Judge's Journal* 48 (3): 28–32.

Reed v. Reed, 404 U.S. 71 (1971).

Rehnquist, William H. 2002. "2001 Year-End Report on the Federal Judiciary." Available at http://www.supremecourt.gov/publicinfo/year-end/2001year-endreport.aspx.

Reingold, Beth, and Jessica Harrell. 2010. "The Impact of Descriptive Representation on Women's Political Engagement: Does Party Matter?" *Political Research Quarterly* 63 (2): 280–294.

"Report of the Special Committee on Judicial Selection and Tenure." 1937. *Annual Report of the American Bar Association* 62:893–897.

Republican Party of Minnesota v. White, 536 U.S. 765 (2002).

Richards, David A. J. 1993. *Conscience and the Constitution: History, Theory, and Law of the Reconstruction Amendments*. Princeton, NJ: Princeton University Press.

Roberts, John G. 2007. "2006 Year-End Report on the Federal Judiciary." Available at http://www.supremecourt.gov/publicinfo/year-end/2006year-endreport.pdf.

Roig-Franzia, Manuel. 2002. "Asian, Hispanic Judges Rare; Despite Minorities' Gains, 2 Groups Underrepresented." *Washington Post*, March 3, p. T06.

Rosenberg, Gerald N. 2008. *The Hollow Hope: Can Courts Bring About Social Change?* Chicago: Chicago University Press.

Rosenberg, Maurice. 1966. "The Qualities of Justices: Are They Strainable?" *Texas Law Review* 44 (6): 1063–1080.

Royster Guano Co. v. Virginia, 53 U.S. 412 (1920).

Rusch, Jonathan J. 1978. "William H. Hastie and the Vindication of Civil Rights." *Howard Law Journal* 21 (3): 749–820.

Russell, Janice D. 2008. "The Merits of Merit Selection." *Kansas Journal of Law and Public Policy* 17 (3): 437–449.

Ryan, Barbara. 1992. *Feminism and the Women's Movement: Dynamics of Change in Social Movement Ideology and Activism*. New York: Routledge.

Salokar, Rebecca Mae, D. Jason Berggren, and Kathryn A. DePalo. 2006. "The New Politics of Judicial Selection in Florida: Merit Selection Redefined." *Justice System Journal* 27 (2): 123–142.

Salomon, Richard A., and Suzanne D. Rubens. 1992. "Making Judicial Selection Make Sense." *Chicago Tribune*, June 6, p. 21.

Sandefur, Rebecca L. 2007. "Lawyers' Pro Bono Service and American-Style Civil Legal Assistance." *Law and Society Review* 41 (1): 79–112.

Sanders, Stacie L. 1995. "Kissing Babies, Shaking Hands, and Campaign Contributions: Is This the Proper Role for the Kansas Judiciary?" *Washburn Law Journal* 34 (3): 573–587.

Schaffner, Brian F., Matthew Streb, and Gerald Wright. 2001. "Terms without Uniforms: The Nonpartisan Ballot in State and Local Elections." *Political Research Quarterly* 54 (1): 7–30.

Scherer, Nancy. 2005. "Blacks on the Bench." *Political Science Quarterly* 119 (4): 655–675.

———. 2011. "Diversifying the Federal Bench: Is Universal Legitimacy for the U.S. Justice System Possible?" *Northwestern University Law Review* 105 (2): 587–633.

Scherer, Nancy, and Brett Curry. 2010. "Does Descriptive Race Representation Enhance Institutional Legitimacy? The Case of the U.S. Courts." *Journal of Politics* 72 (1): 90–104.

Schmalbeck, Richard. 1998. "The Durability of Law School Reputation." *Journal of Legal Education* 48 (4): 568–590.

Schneider, Matthew. 2010. "Why Merit Selection of State Court Judges Lacks Merit." *Wayne Law Review* 56 (2): 609–666.

Schwartz, Bernard. 1997. "Chief Justice Earl Warren: Super Chief in Action." *Tulsa Law Review* 33 (2): 477–503.

Segal, Jeffrey A., and Harold J. Spaeth. 2002. *The Supreme Court and the Attitudinal Model Revisited*. New York: Cambridge University Press.

Sen, Maya. 2014. "How Judicial Qualification Ratings May Disadvantage Minority and Female Candidates." *Journal of Law and Courts* 2 (1): 33–65.

Shafroth, Will. 1934. "The Bar's Opinion on Judicial Selection." *American Bar Association Journal* 20 (9): 529–549.

Shammas, Carole. 1994. "Re-assessing the Married Women's Property Acts." *Journal of Women's History* 6 (1): 9–30.

Sharon, Amiel T., and Craig B. Pettibone. 1987. "Merit Selection of Federal Administrative Law Judges." *Judicature* 70 (4): 216–222.

Sheldon, Charles H. 1968. "Perceptions of the Judicial Roles in Nevada." *Utah Law Review* 1968 (3): 355–368.

Shepherd, Joanna M. 2009a. "Are Appointed Judges Strategic Too?" *Duke Law Journal* 58 (7): 1589–1626.

———. 2009b. "The Influence of Retention Politics on Judges' Voting." *Journal of Legal Studies* 38 (1): 169–206.

———. 2009c. "Money, Politics, and Impartial Justice." *Duke Law Journal* 58 (4): 623–686.

Shortell, Christopher. 2010. "When Justice Is Not Blind: Corruption in the Courts." In *Corruption and American Politics*, edited by Michael A. Genovese and Victoria A. Farrar-Myers, 209–242. Amherst, NY: Cambria Press.

Shugerman, Jed Handelsman. 2010. "Economic Crisis and the Rise of Judicial Elections and Judicial Review." *Harvard Law Review* 123 (5): 1061–1150.

———. 2012. *The People's Courts: Pursuing Judicial Independence in America*. Cambridge, MA: Harvard University Press.

Shuman, Daniel W., and Anthony Champagne. 1997. "Removing the People from the Legal Process: The Rhetoric and Research on Judicial Selection and Juries." *Psychology, Public Policy, and Law* 3 (2–3): 242–258.

Simmons, Ric. 2012. "ChooseYourJudges.org: Treating Elected Judges as Politicians." *Akron Law Review* 45 (1): 1–61.

Sipuel v. Board of Regents of the University of Oklahoma, 332 U.S. 631 (1948).

Sisk, Gregory C., Michael Heise, and Andrew P. Morriss. 1998. "Charting the Influences on the Judicial Mind: An Empirical Study of Judicial Reasoning." *New York University Law Review* 73 (5): 1377–1500.

Slaughter-House Cases, 83 U.S. 36 (1873).

Slotnick, Elliot E. 1983. "Lowering the Bench or Raising It Higher? Affirmative Action and Judicial Selection during the Carter Administration." *Yale Law and Policy Review* 1 (2): 270–298.

———. 1984. "Judicial Selection Systems and Nomination Outcomes: Does the Process Make a Difference?" *American Politics Research* 12 (2): 225–240.

Smelcer, Susan Navarro, Amy Steigerwalt, and Richard L. Vining Jr. 2012. "Bias and the Bar: Evaluating the ABA Ratings of Federal Judicial Nominees." *Political Research Quarterly* 65 (4): 827–840.

Smith, Christopher E. 1987. "Merit Selection Committees and the Politics of Appointing United States Magistrates." *Justice System Journal* 12 (2): 210–231.

Smith, J. Clay, Jr. 1993. *Emancipation: The Making of the Black Lawyer, 1844–1944*. Philadelphia: University of Pennsylvania Press.

———. 1995. "In Freedom's Birthplace: The Making of George Lewis Ruffin, the First Black Law Graduate of Harvard University." *Howard Law Journal* 39 (1): 201–236.

Smith, Malcolm. 1951. "The California Method of Selecting Judges." *Stanford Law Review* 3 (4): 571–600.

Smith, William E. 2010. "Reflections on Judicial Merit Selection, the Rhode Island Experience, and Some Modest Proposals for Reform and Improvement." *Roger Williams University Law Review* 15 (3): 649–659.

Solberg, Rorie Spill. 2005. "Diversity and George W. Bush's Judicial Appointments." *Judicature* 88 (6): 276–283.

Solum, Lawrence B. 2005. "A Tournament of Virtue." *Florida State University Law Review* 32 (4): 1365–1400.

Songer, Donald R., Sue Davis, and Susan Haire. 1994. "A Reappraisal of Diversification in the Federal Courts: Gender Effects in the Courts of Appeals." *Journal of Politics* 56 (2): 425–439.

Sotomayor, Sonia. 2002. "A Latina Judge's Voice." *Berkeley La Raza Law Journal* 13 (1): 87–94.

"Sotomayor Nomination." 2009. *Congressional Record—Senate* 155 (96): S6977–S6985. Available at https://www.congress.gov/crec/2009/06/24/CREC-2009-06-24.pdf.

Southworth, Ann. 2013. "What Is Public Interest Law? Empirical Perspectives on an Old Question." *DePaul Law Review* 62 (2): 493–518.

Spaeth, Harold J., Sara C. Benesh, Lee Epstein, Andrew D. Martin, Jeffrey A. Segal, and Theodore J. Ruger. 2014. *Supreme Court Database.* Available at http://supremecourtdatabase.org.

Spill, Rorie L., and Kathleen A. Bratton. 2000. "Clinton and Diversification of the Federal Judiciary." *Judicature* 84 (5): 256–261.

Squire, Peverill. 2008. "Measuring the Professionalization of U.S. State Courts of Last Resort." *State Politics and Policy Quarterly* 8 (3): 223–238.

Stanford News Service. 2005. "Stanford Community Mourns the Death of William H. Rehnquist '48, MA '48, LLB '52." September 4. Available at http://news.stanford.edu/pr/2005/pr-rehnquist-091405.html.

Stanton v. Stanton, 421 U.S. 7 (1975).

Stith, Laura Denvir, and Jeremy Root. 2009. "The Missouri Nonpartisan Court Plan: The Least Political Method of Selecting High Quality Judges." *Missouri Law Review* 74 (3): 711–750.

Stone, Harlan F. 1934. "The Public Influence of the Bar." *Harvard Law Review* 48 (1): 1–14.

Streb, Matthew J. 2007. "The Study of Judicial Elections." In *Running for Judge: The Rising Political, Financial, and Legal Stakes of Judicial Elections*, edited by Matthew J. Streb, 1–14. New York: New York University Press.

Streb, Matthew J., Brian Frederick, and Casey LaFrance. 2009. "Voter Rolloff in a Low-Information Context: Evidence from Intermediate Appellate Court Elections." *American Politics Research* 37 (4): 644–669.

Strum, Philippa. 1984. *Louis D. Brandeis: Justice for the People.* Cambridge, MA: Harvard University Press.

Sturm, Albert L. 1982. "The Development of American State Constitutions." *Publius: The Journal of Federalism* 12 (1): 57–98.

Surrency, Erwin C. 1967. "The Courts in the American Colonies." *American Journal of Legal History* 11 (3): 253–276.

Sweatt v. Painter, 339 U.S. 629 (1950).

Szmer, John, Robert K. Christensen, and Erin B. Kaheny. 2015. "Gender, Race, and Dissensus on State Supreme Courts." *Social Science Quarterly* 96 (2): 553–575.

Szmer, John, and Martha Humphries Ginn. 2014. "Examining the Effects of Information, Attorney Capability, and Amicus Participation on U.S. Supreme Court Decision Making." *American Politics Research* 42 (3): 441–471.

Tabarrok, Alexander, and Eric Helland. 1999. "Court Politics: The Political Economy of Tort Awards." *Journal of Law and Economics* 42 (1): 157–188.

Taft, William H. 1913. "The Selection and Tenure of Judges." *Annual Report of the American Bar Association* 36:418–435.

Talbott, Basil. 1987. "Court Reform on Road to Nowhere." *Chicago Sun-Times*, May 12, p. 39.

Tarr, G. Alan. 1998. *Understanding State Constitutions*. Princeton, NJ: Princeton University Press.

———. 2003. "Rethinking the Selection of State Supreme Court Justices." *Willamette Law Review* 39 (4): 1445–1470.

———. 2007. "Designing an Appointive System: The Key Issues." *Fordham Urban Law Journal* 34 (1): 291–314.

———. 2009. "Do Retention Elections Work?" *Missouri Law Review* 74 (3): 605–633.

Tate, C. Neal, and Roger Handberg. 1991. "Time Binding and Theory Building in Personal Attribute Models of Supreme Court Voting Behavior, 1916–88." *American Journal of Political Science* 35 (2): 460–488.

Theriault, Sean M. 2003. "Patronage, the Pendleton Act, and the Power of the People." *Journal of Politics* 65 (1): 50–68.

Tobias, Carl. 1993. "Rethinking Federal Judicial Selection." *Brigham Young University Law Review* 1993 (4): 1257–1286.

———. 2013. "Senate Gridlock and Federal Judicial Selection." *Notre Dame Law Review* 88 (5): 2233–2266.

Tokarz, Karen L. 1986. "Women Judges and Merit Selection under the Missouri Plan." *Washington University Law Quarterly* 64 (3): 903–952.

Tolbert, Pamela S., and Lynne G. Zucker. 1983. "Institutional Sources of Change in the Formal Structure of Organizations: The Diffusion of Civil Service Reform, 1880–1935." *Administrative Science Quarterly* 28 (1): 22–39.

Uehlein, Julius, and David H. Wilderman. 2002. "Why Merit Selection Is Inconsistent with Democracy." *Dickinson Law Review* 106 (4): 769–772.

United States v. Pendergast, 28 F. Supp. 601 (1939).

United States v. Yazell, 382 U.S. 341 (1966).

Vandenberg, Donna. 1983. "Voluntary Merit Selection: Its History and Current Status." *Judicature* 66 (5): 265–278.

Vermeule, Adrian. 2007. "Should We Have Lay Justices?" *Stanford Law Review* 59 (6): 1569–1611.

Vile, John R., and Mario Perez-Reilly. 1991. "The U.S. Constitution and Judicial Qualifications: A Curious Omission." *Judicature* 74 (4): 198–202.

Vining, Richard L., Jr., and Teena Wilhelm. 2011. "Measuring Case Salience in State Courts of Last Resort." *Political Research Quarterly* 64 (3): 559–572.

Vining, Richard L., Jr., Teena Wilhelm, Sara E. Hiers, and Phil Marcin. 2010. "Patterns of Newspaper Reporting on State Supreme Courts." *Justice System Journal* 31 (3): 273–289.

Volcansek, Mary L., and Jacqueline Lucienne Lafon. 1988. *Judicial Selection: The Cross-Evolution of French and American Practices*. New York: Greenwood.

Ward, Artemus, and David L. Weiden. 2006. *Sorcerers' Apprentices: 100 Years of Law Clerks at the United States Supreme Court*. New York: New York University Press.

Ware, Stephen J. 2008. "Selection to the Kansas Supreme Court." *Kansas Journal of Law and Public Policy* 17 (3): 386–423.

———. 2009. "The Missouri Plan in National Perspective." *Missouri Law Review* 74 (3): 751–775.

———. 2015. "Judicial Elections, Judicial Impartiality and Legitimate Judicial Lawmaking: *Williams-Yulee v. The Florida Bar.*" *Vanderbilt Law Review En Banc* 68:59–81.

Waterman, Sterry R. 1963. "The 50th Year of the American Judicature Society." *Journal of the American Judicature Society* 47 (3): 44–45.

Watson, James L. 1987. "The Afro-American and the Constitution: Colonial Times to Present." *Maine Law Review* 39 (2): 267–274.

Watson, Richard A., and Rondal G. Downing. 1969. *The Politics of the Bench and the Bar: Judicial Selection under the Missouri Nonpartisan Court Plan.* New York: John Wiley and Sons.

Weisberg, D. Kelly. 1977. "Barred from the Bar: Women and Legal Education in the United States, 1870–1890." *Journal of Legal Education* 28 (4): 485–507.

Welch, Susan, Michael Combs, and John Gruhl. 1988. "Do Black Judges Make a Difference?" *American Journal of Political Science* 32 (1): 126–136.

Wheat, Elizabeth, and Mark S. Hurwitz. 2013. "The Politics of Judicial Selection: The Case of the Michigan Supreme Court." *Judicature* 96 (4): 178–188.

Wheeler, Russell. 2010. "Changing Backgrounds of U.S. District Judges: Likely Causes and Possible Implications." *Judicature* 93 (4): 140–149.

White, Adam J. 2005. "Toward the Framers' Understanding of Advice and Consent: A Historical and Textual Inquiry." *Harvard Journal of Law and Public Policy* 29 (1): 103–148.

White, G. Edward. 2012. *Law in American History.* Vol. 1, *From the Colonial Years through the Civil War.* New York: Oxford University Press.

Williams, Juan. 1998. *Thurgood Marshall: American Revolutionary.* New York: Random House.

Williams, Laurens. 1953. "The President's Message." *Nebraska State Bar Journal* 2 (1): 5–9.

Williams, Margaret. 2007. "Women's Representation on State Trial and Appellate Courts." *Social Science Quarterly* 88 (5): 1192–1204.

Williams, Richard. 2010. "Fitting Heterogeneous Choice Models with OGLM." *Stata Journal* 10 (4): 540–567.

Williams-Yulee v. The Florida Bar, 135 S. Ct. 1656 (2015).

Wingfield, Kyle. 2009. "State High Court Shifts to the Right." *Atlanta Journal-Constitution*, September 3, p. 14A.

Winslow, John B. 1917. "The Property Rights of Married Women under Modern Laws (Part II)." *Marquette Law Review* 1 (2): 53–64.

Winters, Glenn R. 1966. "Selection of Judges: An Historical Introduction." *Texas Law Review* 44 (6): 1081–1087.

———. 1968. "The Merit Plan for Judicial Selection and Tenure: It's Historical Development." *Duquesne Law Review* 7 (1): 61–78.

———. 1972. "Merit Selection of Federal Judges." *Kentucky Law Journal* 60 (4): 872–884.

Wolak, Jennifer. 2014. "Candidate Gender and the Political Engagement of Women and Men." *American Politics Research* 43 (5): 872–896.

Wood, Fred B., ed. 1934. *Proposed Amendments to Constitution, Propositions and Proposed Laws.* Sacramento: California State Printing Office.

Wood, Gordon S. 1993. "Foreword: State Constitution-Making in the American Revolution." *Rutgers Law Journal* 24 (4): 911–926.

Wood, John Perry. 1937. "Basic Propositions Relating to Judicial Selection: Failure of Direct Primary—Appointment through Dual Agency—Judge to 'Run on Record.'" *American Bar Association Journal* 23 (2): 102–105.

———. 1938. "Elements of Judicial Selection." *American Bar Association Journal* 24 (7): 541–544.

———. 1943. "Missouri Victory Speeds National Judicial Selection Reform." *Journal of the American Judicature Society* 26 (5): 142–144.

Woodward, C. Vann. 2002. *The Strange Career of Jim Crow.* New York: Oxford University Press.

Woody, R. H. 1933. "Jonathan Jasper Wright, Associate Justice of the Supreme Court of South Carolina, 1870–77." *Journal of Negro History* 18 (2): 114–131.

Worrall, John L. 2008. "Prosecution in America: A Historical and Comparative Account." In *The Changing Role of the American Prosecutor*, edited by John Worrall and M. Elaine Nugent-Borakove, 3–30. Albany: State University of New York Press.

Wright, Ronald F. 2009. "How Prosecutor Elections Fail Us." *Ohio State Journal of Criminal Law* 6 (2): 581–610.

Yarbrough, Tinsley E. 2005. *David Hackett Souter: Traditional Republican on the Rehnquist Court.* New York: Oxford University Press.

Yelnosky, Michael J. 2010. "The Impact of Merit Selection on the Characteristics of Rhode Island Judges." *Roger Williams University Law Review* 15 (3): 649–659.

Zaccari, Laura. 2004. "Judicial Elections: Recent Developments, Historical Perspective, and Continued Viability." *Richmond Journal of Law and the Public Interest* 8 (1): 138–156.

Zackin, Emily. 2013. *Looking for Rights in All the Wrong Places: Why State Constitutions Contain America's Positive Rights.* Princeton, NJ: Princeton University Press.

Zeidman, Steven. 2005. "Judicial Politics: Making the Case for Merit Selection." *Albany Law Review* 68 (3): 713–722.

Zeisberg, Mariah. 2009. "Should We Elect the US Supreme Court?" *Perspectives on Politics* 7 (4): 785–803.

Ziskind, Martha Andres. 1969. "Judicial Tenure in the American Constitution: English and American Precedents." *Supreme Court Review* 1969:135–154.

Zorn, Christopher, and Jennifer Barnes Bowie. 2010. "Ideological Influences on Decision Making in the Federal Judicial Hierarchy." *Journal of Politics* 72 (4): 1212–1221.

INDEX

Greg Goelzhauser is an Assistant Professor of Political Science at Utah State University.